Creative Kids
Complete
Photo Guide to

Sewing

First published in the United States of America by
Creative Publishing international, a division of
Quarto Publishing Group USA Inc.
400 First Avenue North
Suite 400
Minneapolis, MN 55401
1-800-328-3895
www.creativepub.com
Visit www.Craftside.net for a behind-the-scenes peek
at our crafty world!

ISBN: 978-1-58923-823-7

10 9 8 7 6 5 4 3 2 1

Library of Congress Cataloging-in-Publication Data available
Copy Editor: Karen Levy
Design and Layout: Laura McFadden Design, Inc.
Photography: Brylye Collins Photography, Glenn Scott
Photography, Toni Hamel Photography

Printed in China

Creative Kids

Complete
Photo Guide to
Sewing

Janith Bergeron
Christine Ecker

Creative Publishing
international

contents

Introduction

Have you ever been having *sew* much fun you didn't realize you were building your skills? Join us as we take you from the basics of hand stitching to the fun of machine sewing and off to the world of creative design! As you are learning new skills you will be making projects that are exciting and fun. Once you learn the basics, you can add your own design elements and embellishments, which increase not only your knowledge and skills, but the fun factor as well! When you become comfortable sewing simple projects, you will then move on to creating items just for you!

We are offering a unique view of sewing, which needs your creativity and imagination to see how far you can go. A simple task of stitching a chenille pot holder can expand into making a chenille rug for your pet—or even one for your room! Each project will begin with a basic idea with detailed directions and photographs. We will explain the materials and tools that you will need, the skills you should know before beginning the project, and the skills you will learn. After completing "our" version, think of how to expand, change, or embellish it. Your imagination will become the focus as you move through the book and build your skills and confidence.

Your job is to believe in yourself. We ask that you learn about the tools you will need, the machine you will use, and how to organize your sewing tools. We will teach you how to be safe while using the machine and sewing tools. All the techniques and know-how can be learned in this book while having fun.

The more you know, the more fun it is to sew.

The more you sew, the more you will know!

Sewing Safely

As you begin to sew, you will be using tools that, perhaps, you have never seen or used before. Although we will describe the correct way to use these tools and give you tips on safety, it will be up to you and your parents to discuss what they feel comfortable with you using—whether it will be alone, with adult supervision, or with adult assistance. It is important to keep in mind that many of these tools are pointy, sharp, or hot, and you will need to remain focused as you use them. Always ask for help if you are unsure.

How to Use This Book

As you begin using this book and learning to sew, it will help if you understand how it is set up. We will begin with Hand Sewing, move on to Machine Sewing, and finish with Creative Design and making garments for *your* body. Each chapter will introduce the tools and skills that are involved with that particular section while building on skills already learned. There will be several projects in each section, and they will range from easiest to more challenging. Furthermore, each project will have suggestions and tips on how to make it your own through embellishment and design.

Because, like you, we want to get to the "fun stuff" quickly, we have put the "dry stuff" in the back, where you will be able to find it easily when you need it. That is not to say that we are skipping over any information you need to know, but by putting it all together in the Appendix, it will be accessible when you need it.

Throughout this book are tips that will explain special methods and offer ideas or refer you to a page in the appendix where you can learn more. We hope you find this system easy to use so all the information you need is at your fingertips.

Hand sewing is a great way to begin learning how to handle needles, threads, and fabrics. You will begin with two projects that will introduce several of the basic hand stitches: backstitch, cross-stitch, blanket stitch, and slip stitch. For both of your hand projects you will be working on felt, but you could easily use felted wool instead. It is important that you get a good-quality felt so that your project will hold up and be easier to stitch on. Stay away from very thin, floppy felt. Felt is a nice first fabric because it has a bit of body, which makes it easier to hold, and it does not ravel, so no seam finish will be needed. You will be using crewel or chenille needles, both of which have points sharp enough to easily go through the felt and eyes large enough to accommodate the embroidery floss you will be using for thread. You will be using all six strands together and not separating them like you may do in some handwork.

Getting Started

XXXXXXXXXXXXXXXXXXXXXXXXXXXXXXXXXXXXXXXXXX

Let's learn some basics and safety first. Needles and pins are sharp and small, so you need to handle them carefully and keep track of them. Always remember to put your needles and pins in a piece of fabric or in a needle holder when you are not using them. When you are hand sewing, make sure you have plenty of room so you don't accidentally poke anyone or yourself with the needle.

Threading a sewing needle with regular thread and threading a large eye needle with floss are two different things. Let's take a look at both.

 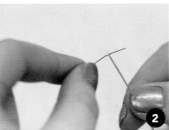

Threading a Sewing Needle with Thread

1 Cut a fresh end of thread to make it go through the eye of the needle easier.

2 Hold the thread close to the end so that thread end bends less. Place the end through the eye of the needle and pull through.

Threading a Large-Eye Needle with Floss

1 Fold the floss over the eye end of the needle, pinch it together tightly, and slide it off the needle.

2 Keeping the floss pinched between your thumb and forefinger, guide the eye of the needle over the thread, forcing the floss through the eye. Grasp the pinched thread and pull through the eye completely.

3 **Optional** You may also use a needle threader if you are having trouble getting the thread through the eye.

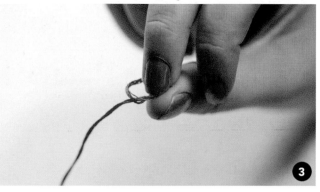

Tying a Knot at the End of Thread

1 If you are using a double strand of thread, you will be tying both ends together and will need to even up the thread ends. If you are sewing with a single strand, you will tie a knot in only one thread end and leave the other end loose. The actual knot tying is the same.

2 Loop the thread snugly around your index or middle finger, holding it in place with your thumb.

3 Roll the thread off your finger, keeping the tension tight and holding it in place with your thumb.

4 Keeping your thumb and finger together, gently pull the thread. This will give you a double knot in your thread.

Tying Off the Last Stitch

1 At the end of your seam, you will need to secure your stitches by tying off your thread. With regular thread or floss, take one short stitch close to the end, leaving a loop to put the needle through.

2 Pull the thread snugly and repeat with another stitch right on top of the previous stitch.

3 Cut the thread end close to the fabric.

With these things in mind, you can now move on to your first project!

45-60
minutes

Flower Power Needle Holder

What a fun way to store your needles! This adorable Flower Power Needle Holder is made from felt, buttons, and embroidery floss. Store your needles safely between the petals, with the button closed to keep them contained. Use different petals to hold different sizes/types of needles! Once you've completed this project, use felt and blanket stitch to make a needle book for your sewing machine needles.

You Will Need

Tools

- pins
- scissors
- hem gauge
- marking pencil
- crewel or chenille hand needle

Fabric

- two 11" x 11" (28 x 28 cm) squares of yellow felt
- one 3" x 7" (7.5 x 18 cm) piece of blue felt

Other Supplies

- embroidery floss
- one large button 1½" (3.8 cm)
- five ⅝" (1.6 cm) buttons

Patterns

- petal (page 135)
- flower center

You already know

- How to thread an embroidery needle
- How to tie a knot

You will learn

- How to trace, mark, and cut a pattern
- How to sew a button on
- How to sew a blanket stitch

Directions

1 Pin the Petal pattern to two layers of yellow felt and cut out. Pin the Circle pattern to two layers of blue felt and cut out.

2 On the back of the top layer of petals, use the hem gauge and pencil to measure down ½" (1.3 cm) from the tip of each petal and then draw a ½" (1.3 cm) line to mark each buttonhole.

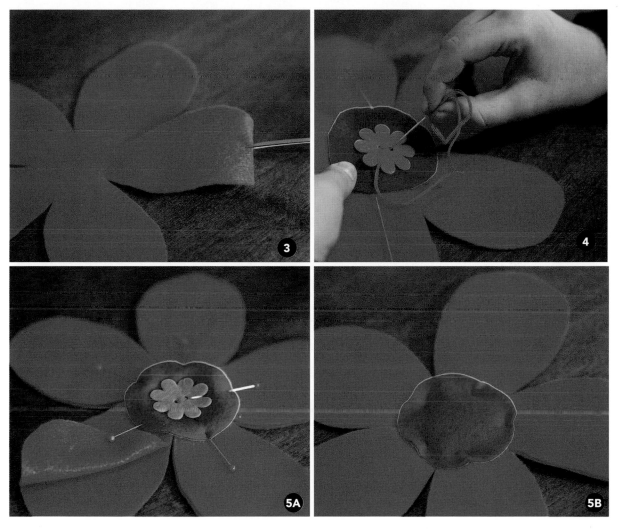

3 Using sharp scissors, cut a slit along each marked line to create buttonholes.

Tip It's better to cut the slit too small and have to enlarge it, rather than too big and thus too loose.

4 Center a blue circle on one layer of yellow petals and pin. Thread a crewel needle with six strands of embroidery floss and tie a knot at the end (page 11). Center the large button on the blue circle. Bring the needle up from the back, through one hole of the button. Then go down through the other hole. Repeat with one more stitch through the button holes, and tie off the thread on the back.

5 Pin both flower petals together with the blue circle on top and add the second blue circle to the center back (A, B).

6 Thread the needle again with six strands of embroidery floss and tie a knot at the end.

(continued)

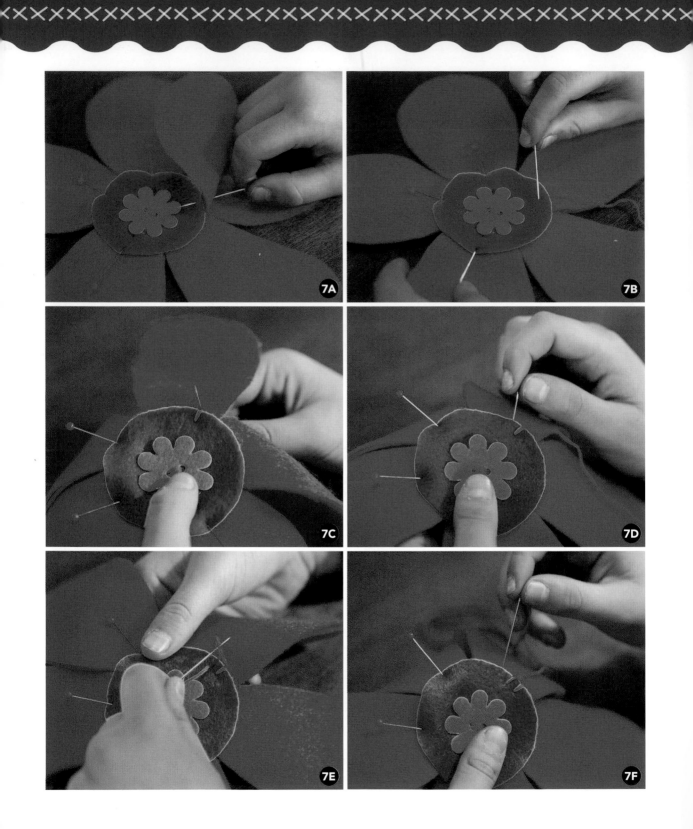

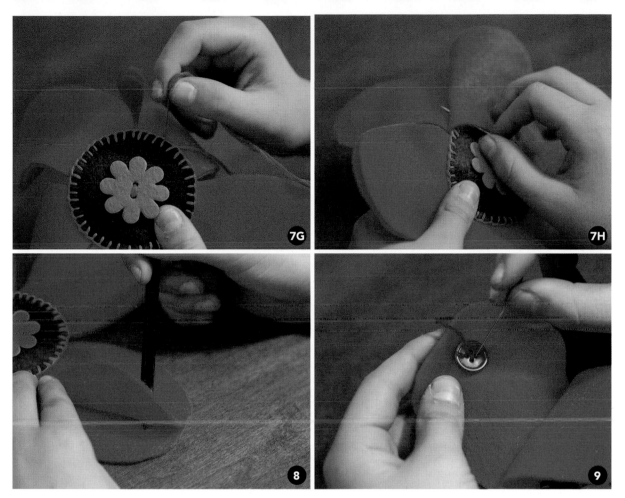

7 Secure the circles using blanket stitch, following these directions. Insert the needle between two layers of petals to hide the knot. For the first stitch, come up just outside the blue circle (A). Go down ⅛" (3 mm) inside the blue circle through all the layers of fabric (B). Come back up to the first hole just outside the blue circle (C). To begin the next stitch, go down just outside of the blue circle, ⅛" (3 mm) away, and come up ⅛" (3 mm) inside the blue circle. Pull the thread through, leaving a loop (D). Stick the needle through the loop (D) and gently tug the stitch into place. Go down just outside of the blue circle, ⅛" (3 mm) away, beginning the next stitch (F). Repeat all the way around. To finish, insert the needle into the same beginning hole as the first stitch (G), pulling the needle out between two petals (H), and tie a knot so it is hidden between the petals. .

8 Using a pencil, make a dot on the bottom petal layer through each buttonhole to mark the placement for the buttons.

9 Using six strands of embroidery floss and the crewel needle, stitch the buttons on in an X pattern, tying off in back.

45-60
minutes
without
embellishments

Tooth Fairy Pillow

How exciting to lose a tooth! Now you can create your own very special place to safely tuck your tooth away while waiting for the tooth fairy to arrive! This tooth-shaped pillow has a small pocket on the front to hold a note or your tooth. Use some simple embroidery stitches to personalize your pillow. Once you've mastered this pillow, use your imagination to create different shaped pillows.

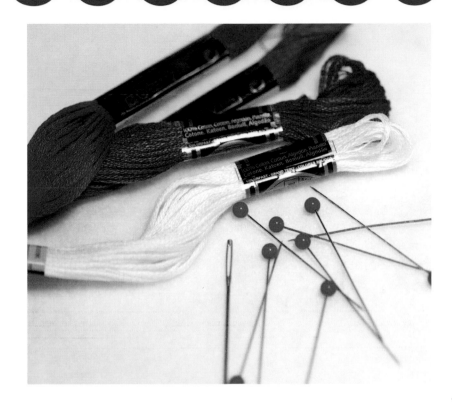

You will need

Tools

- pins
- marking pencil
- scissors
- crewel or chenille needle
- point turner

Fabric

- two 14" x 14" (35.5 x 35.5 cm) squares of heavyweight white felt

Other Supplies

- white embroidery floss
- colored embroidery floss (optional)
- stuffing

Patterns

- tooth
- pocket
- small tooth

You already know

- How to trace, mark, and cut out a pattern
- How to thread a needle
- How to tie a knot

You will learn

- Embroidery stitches: cross-stitch, backstitch
- Sewing stitches: slip stitch
- How to transfer marks from a pattern to the fabric

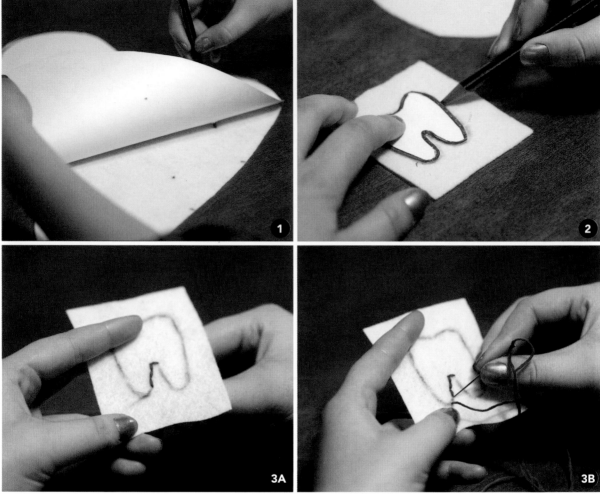

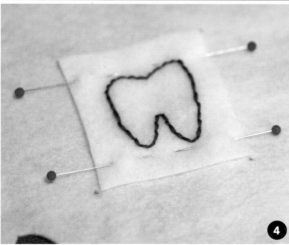

Directions

1 Pin the pattern for the tooth pillow onto two layers of white felt and trace with a marking pencil. Cut out the pillow pieces. Transfer the markings for the opening and pocket placement onto the top layer of felt (the pillow front).

2 Pin the pocket pattern onto one layer of white felt, trace, and cut out. Lightly trace the small tooth onto the center of the pocket

3 Thread a needle with six strands of embroidery floss, and knot the end. Stitch the outline of the tooth using back stitch. Bring the needle up from the back anywhere along the line. Insert the needle a short distance behind (to the right), and pull

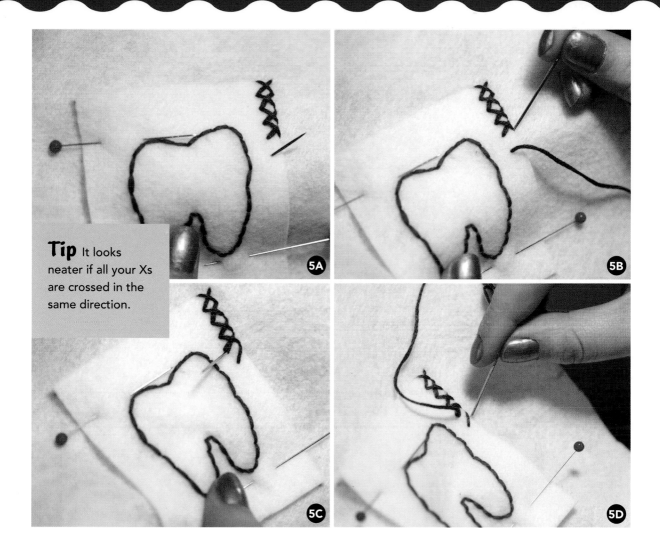

Tip It looks neater if all your Xs are crossed in the same direction.

5A

5B

5C

5D

through. Bring the needle back to the front a stitch-length ahead (to the left) of the first stitch. Repeat these steps, continuing along the line, until the entire tooth is outlined. Tie off the thread on the back.

4 Pin the pocket onto the pillow front at the placement marks.

5 Thread a needle with six strands of embroidery floss, and knot the ends. Beginning in an upper corner, use cross-stitch to attach the pocket to the pillow. Bring the needle up from the back about ⅛" (3 mm) in from the side and down from the top right corner of the pocket. Insert the needle back into the fabric at the corner (one diagonal stitch completed). Bring the needle up at the top of the pocket in line with the bottom of the first diagonal stitch. Insert the needle back into the fabric at the side of the pocket in line with the bottom of the first diagonal stitch (one cross stitch completed). Now think of your next X. Bring the needle up from the back at the bottom left of the next X (A). Make the diagonal stitch to the outside edge of the pocket, inserting the needle into the same hole as bottom right of the previous X (B). Bring the needle up from the back in the same hole as the bottom left of the previous X (C). Complete the cross stitch with the second diagonal stitch (D). Repeat all around the pocket. Tie off the thread at the back.

(continued)

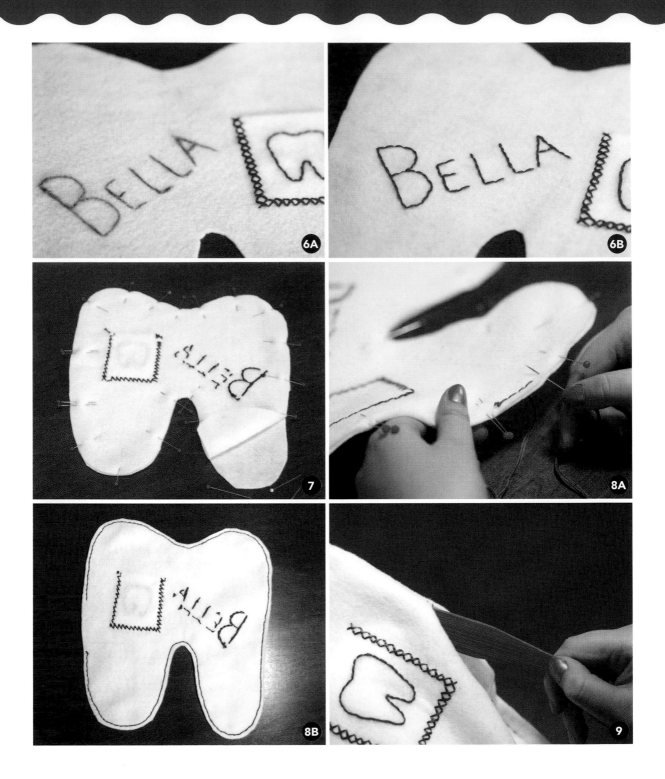

6 If you would like to stitch a name on the pillow, lightly write the letters on the front of the pillow, staying at least ¾" (2 cm) away from the edges (A). Use backstitch to follow the writing and embroider the name (B).

7 Pin the pillow front to the pillow back with right sides together (the pocket will be sandwiched between the layers of the pillow). Mark the opening with double pins.

8 Using white embroidery floss, begin at one end of the opening mark and use a backstitch ⅛" (3 mm) away from the edge to stitch all the way around the edge of the pillow until you come to the other opening mark (A). Tie off to end (B). (We used blue floss in the photo so you could see it better.)

9 Turn the pillow right side out through the opening and use the rounded side of the point turner to smooth the curves.

(continued)

Tips Tie off each letter so the connecting thread does not show through.

Place two pins close together at each end of the opening to easily see where to begin and end.

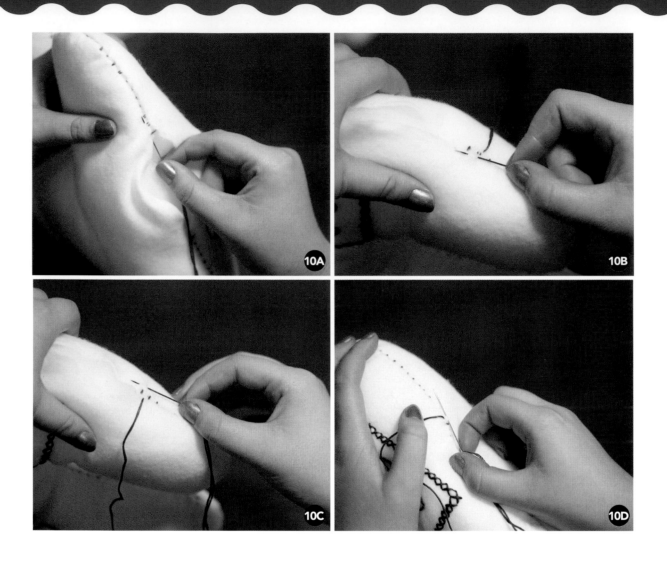

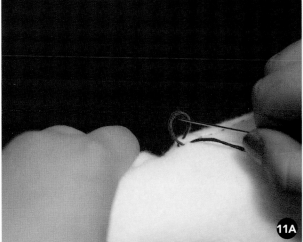

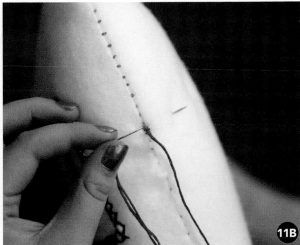

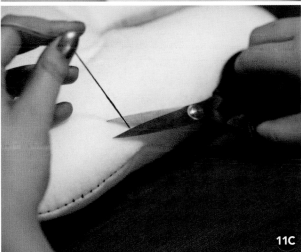

10 Stuff the pillow through the opening until the desired fullness is reached. Close the opening with slip stitches, following these instructions. Thread the needle with white embroidery floss and knot the end. Bring the needle up in the seam line just BEFORE the opening (A). Insert the needle ⅛" (3 mm) from the edge in the opposite side of the opening directly across from the previous stitch and take a small stich (B). Take another small stich opposite the previous stitch and pull the stitches tight. The raw edges will fold to the inside (C). Continue taking small stitches, crossing from one side of the opening to the other until you are just PAST the opening (D).

11 Take a tiny stitch and tie a knot (A). Stick the needle through the seam, pull the needle out through the pillow (B), and snip close to the fabric (C). When relaxed, the thread end will retreat into the pillow and will not be seen.

Machine Sewing

XXX ×××××××××××××××××××××××××

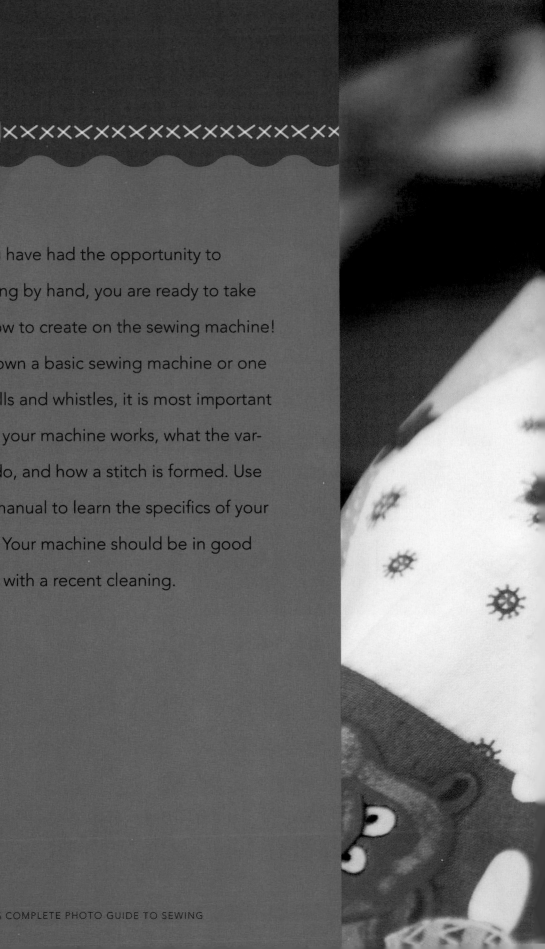

Now that you have had the opportunity to explore stitching by hand, you are ready to take on learning how to create on the sewing machine! Whether you own a basic sewing machine or one with all the bells and whistles, it is most important to learn HOW your machine works, what the various settings do, and how a stitch is formed. Use your owner's manual to learn the specifics of your own machine. Your machine should be in good working order with a recent cleaning.

Getting to Know Your Machine

 First, identify key parts to your machine and understand how they work. Sit at your machine with your owner's manual and refer to the Appendix in the back of this book entitled "Sewing Machine" to explore the parts of your machine and see how they move. It is best if you do this with a machine that is not threaded so that you will not run into tangles and can focus more clearly on the machine itself. Obviously, when you get to threading the machine and seeing how a stitch is formed you will need to thread your machine. If you do not have a manual, most can be downloaded from the Internet. Remember that proper maintenance and frequent cleaning of your machine will keep it running smoothly, which will translate into more fun for you!

Once you have explored your machine parts, practiced using your foot pedal, wound a bobbin, and threaded your machine, it is time to talk about putting it all together!

To keep the fun up front, we have designed a super reference for you in the back of this book. If you come across something you are not familiar with or wish to know more about, chances are it will be in the Appendix: information on the sewing machine, a tool kit, and understanding fabrics and fibers are at your fingertips. Taking a quick walk through these pages will allow you to get up and running with the fewest problems.

Let's practice some stitching on paper and learn some basic techniques. Then you can move on to the first project.

Tips for Success

- When you start to sew a seam, make sure your thread tails are under the presser foot and that your presser foot is down.

- ALWAYS make sure the take-up lever is in the highest position when you begin and end a seam! Three clues the take-up lever is not at its highest point:

    A The fabric is hard to pull out of the machine.

    B More than two threads are attached to the fabric.

    C The needle keeps coming unthreaded.

- Press your foot pedal slowly to start so that your thread is not jerked quickly, which may cause it to get looped around something.

- If you have to reverse, stop your machine completely and press your reverse button firmly to change directions. You will usually need to hold your reverse button down the whole time you wish to sew backward.

- Remember your feed dogs! They are there to move the fabric through your machine. Your job is to steer and keep things where you want them.

- If your machine is making strange noises, stop and make sure it is threaded and sewing properly.

- If you are having a hard time staying on your seam line, you can use a magnetic seam guide or a piece of low-tack tape (such as painter's tape) to help you. *Do not use a magnetic guide on a computerized machine!*

- If you turn your fabric over and see many loops along your seam line, generally that means your bobbin is not in correctly. Sometimes it means the machine is not correctly threaded through all the tension guides and take-up lever.

- Remember that stitching takes practice and embrace it, even if it involves unstitching. Your seam ripper is your friend!

Safety Tip

When you change broken or dull needles or discard bent pins or dull rotary blades, *don't* throw them in the trash! Put them in a lidded container—a small box or jar—that you can keep in your sewing room. When the container is full, cover it and throw it away.

As long as you want

Paper Stitching Practice

Are you ready and excited to get started? These first exercises will help you become more comfortable and proficient at the sewing machine. You will be working on paper without the machine threaded, learning some of the language of sewing, and practicing controlling your machine. Practicing without thread at first allows you to focus on the process without worrying about any thread tangles or other issues.

Dry Run

Directions

NOTES: For safety reasons, when you are not sewing, keep your foot off the pedal. Sometimes, when you are adjusting your fabric and lining things up, you can accidentally lean on the foot pedal, making the machine run, and you don't want your fingers to be near the needle if this happens.

1 First, let's look at posture and machine positioning. Proper posture at the machine is important not only for your body but also for the quality of your stitching. Sit centered in front of the needle so that you can clearly see your seam allowances and more easily direct your fabric. Sit up straight and try not to lean on the table with your forearms or elbows because this limits the motion of your hands and can make your stitching "jerky." Place your foot pedal a comfortable distance away from you where you can reach it and press without lifting your heel off the floor. Try sewing barefoot or in soft-soled shoes so that you can more easily feel the pedal, and thus have more control over your sewing.

2 With your hands in your lap, practice pressing the pedal to go slower and faster. Keep your heel on the floor to anchor your foot and control your speed better. When you want to take just a stitch or two, rest your foot on the pedal and just curl your big toe. Sit on the edge of your chair if it helps you reach the pedal. If you still have a hard time reaching the pedal correctly, then it is okay to put the pedal on a box. When you feel you have control over the pedal, you are ready to move on to practice on paper.

You already know

- How to thread the machine and insert the bobbin
- How to run your machine

You will learn

- How to properly feed paper or fabric through the machine
- How to maintain steady hand pressure
- How to sew a straight line
- How to backtack
- How to sew a curved line

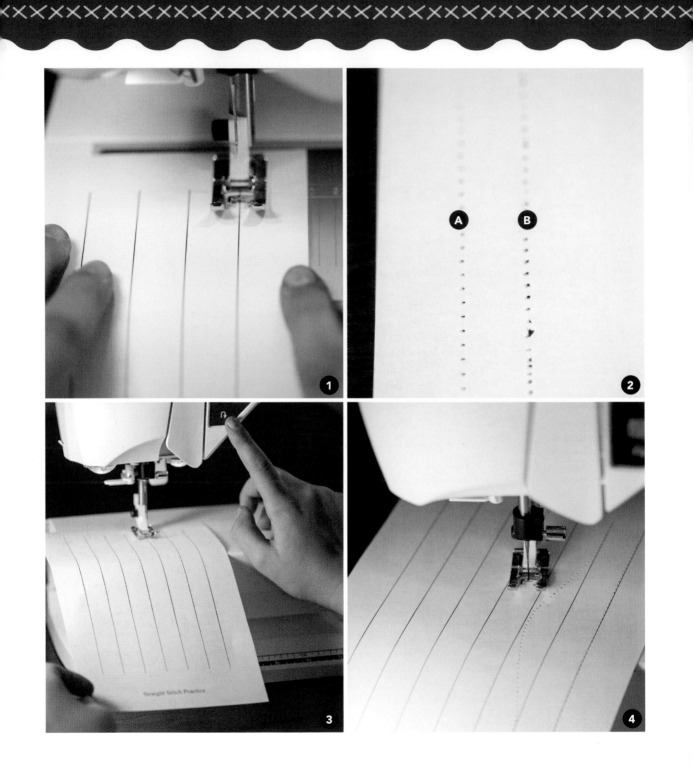

Straight Stitching

Directions

1 Copy the template on page 132. Lift your presser foot and line up your paper so that the first line is centered at your needle. Lower your presser foot. You will complete this first line without using your hands! Your machine may or may not stay on the line, but that will not matter. With hands in your lap, gently press your foot pedal and sew to the end of the line. Take your foot off the pedal and turn the handwheel toward you until the thread take-up lever and needle are in their highest position. Lift your presser foot and remove the paper. Turn your paper over to see what kinds of holes were made. Your paper should have round, evenly spaced holes where your needle has sewn. This will be your goal when you begin to put your hands on the paper to steer.

2 Line up your paper on the next line. This time put your hands lightly on the paper to steer it. Keep your hands in front of the needle to steer from the front instead of pulling from the back. Keep your eye just in front of the presser foot to make sure you have time to make adjustments if needed. Gently press your foot pedal and stitch from the top of the line to the bottom, trying to stay on the line. No fair lifting your presser foot and moving your paper over if you get off the line! Try to gently steer back on if you drift off. Remove the paper and turn it over to look at the holes. If your hand pressure was good, your holes should be round and even (A). If you have too much hand pressure or are pulling your paper instead of gently steering, your holes will be distorted, uneven, and much closer together (B).

3 On the next line you will learn how to backtack. Backtacking prevents the beginning and ending stitches from coming loose. To backtack, start down just a bit from the beginning point and reverse two or three stitches, then stitch forward to sew your seam. When you get to the end, backtack by reversing two or three stitches to secure.

4 Line up your needle on the next line and you will learn how to steer with a practice curve. Stitch a short distance, then start to curve off to the right until you touch the line next to it, and then steer back onto your original line. After you have practiced this direction, do a line or two curving off to the left. These are important to practice until you are comfortable with steering to where you want to go. Remember to check your holes on the back of the paper to learn more about your hand pressure and whether you are tugging the paper into position (uneven, distorted holes) or steering it (even, round holes).

Tip ALWAYS check to make sure your take-up lever and needle are in their highest position before lifting the presser foot and removing paper or fabric. If they are not in the highest position, turn the handwheel toward you until they are.

Pivot

When you need to change the direction of your stitch line at an angle, you need to pivot. Before lifting the presser foot to turn, it is important to anchor the paper (or fabric) by lowering the needle into it. For this exercise, make a copy of the pivot practice sheet on page 133.

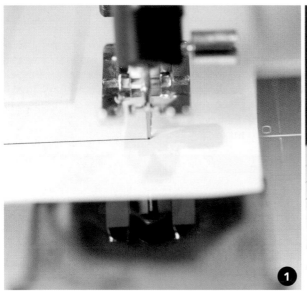

Tip When the beginning and end of your stitching line will meet, rather than back-tack at beginning and end, blend your stitching line by overlapping three stitches.

Directions

1 Line up your paper so that you are starting in the middle of a line for the outer box. Begin by stitching down to the corner of the box and stop with your needle down directly in the corner. It's a good idea to take the last couple of stitches by turning your handwheel toward you so you don't go too far. Leave the needle down in the paper to anchor it in place as you lift the presser foot.

2 Rotate the paper to align with next line of the box. Lower the presser foot.

3 Continue stitching until you reach the next corner, then pivot and repeat until you have stitched all the way around the box and are back where you started. Take three more stitches over the beginning stitches to secure the beginning and end of the line. Turn the handwheel until the take-up lever and needle are at their highest positions, and remove the paper from the machine.

4 Practice on the inner boxes until you feel comfortable with pivoting.

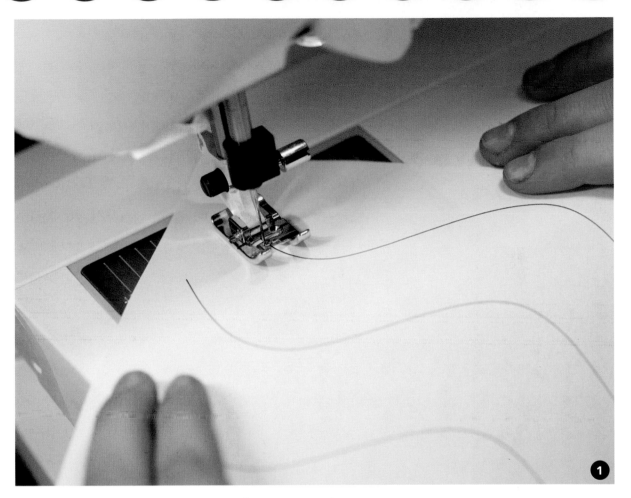

Stitching Curves

Directions

Tip Never lift your presser foot in the middle of a seam without first lowering the needle into the fabric to anchor it. Turn the handwheel toward you until the needle is all the way into the fabric.

1   Make a copy of the slow curve practice sheet (page 134). Start at the beginning of one line and stitch slowly down the line using your hands to steer. The faster you go, the more difficult it will be to stay on the line. These lines are curved gently enough that you should not have to decrease your stitch length, but as the curves get tighter, a shorter stitch length will help you stay on the line. If you stray off the curve, use a series of small pivets to get back on track.

2   Remember to check your holes on the back after each line to see whether you are pushing or pulling too hard.

Scrappy Cards

Once you are comfortable with the practice exercises, thread up your machine and have some fun stitching scraps of fabric to cardstock. These creative, free-form cards are fun to make and share.

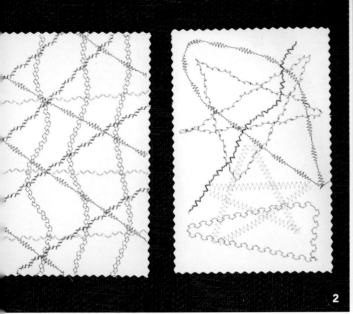

Directions

1 Thread your machine and ready it for sewing by making sure that the bobbin thread is pulled up and both threads are under the presser foot. Each time you start and stop a seam, check to make sure the take-up lever is in the uppermost position.

2 Cut a 5" x 7" (12.5 x 17.8 cm) piece of cardstock. Practice your stitching while making cool designs. Remember: Even though it is paper, you still need to pay attention to the position of the take-up lever and all the basics you just learned to be successful! Backtack at the beginning and end of seams to keep them secure. Try different stitches!

3 Take a 5" x 7" (12.5 x 17.8 cm) piece of cardstock and some scraps of fabric. Stitch the scraps of fabric to the cardstock. You can overlap fabrics and change threads if you want. You can use your pinking shears to cut the edges of fabric scraps to reduce fraying. Be creative and have some fun!

You will need

Tools

- size 80/12 needle
- scissors
- pinking shears

Fabric

- scraps of fabric

Other Supplies

- cotton/polyester thread
- cardstock

You already know

- How to run your machine
- How to maintain steady hand pressure
- How to sew a straight line
- How to backtack
- How to sew a curved line

You will learn

- How to have a little creative fun

1½ hours

Chenille Pot Holder

Here's a great opportunity to use up fabric scraps or "ugly" fabric in the layers. Pick a pretty fabric for the top and bottom, one piece of flannel, and six layers of cotton. Once you've mastered the pot holder, create larger pieces for a table runner or a fun rug.

Directions

This project is designed to use up cotton fabric on hand because the inside pieces do not have to match. You can recycle cotton shirts, too. Use only fabrics that can withstand high heat and will not melt.

Rotary cutters are very sharp! Use only with adult supervision. Please refer to page 124 for further instruction on rotary cutters.

1 Choose your fabrics and organize your tools.

(continued)

You will need

Tools

- size 90/14 needle
- ruler
- rotary cutter and mat (optional)
- marking chalk or pencil
- fabric shears
- pinking shears or rotary cutter with pinking blade
- pins

Fabric

- six 8" x 8" (20 x 20 cm) pieces of cotton (two pretty ones for top and bottom, four others for inside)
- two 8" x 8" (20 x 20 cm) pieces of muslin
- one 8" x 8" (20 x 20 cm) piece of flannel

Other Supplies

- all-purpose thread
- rickrack or ribbon for the holder

You already know

- How to stitch a straight seam
- How to backtack

You will learn

- How to make ½" (1.3 cm) channels
- How to make chenille

1-1½
hours

Funky Fabric Frame

This funky fabric frame is a breeze to make and has many opportunities for personalizing. For example, you can vary the width of the strips, place the strips at different angles, use the photo cutout area to allow for different strip arrangements, topstitch with decorative stitches, or add trims or ribbons. Use this technique to make a base fabric for other projects, such as place mats or room decorations. It's a great project for using up those scraps and a super gift idea.

You will need

Tools

- size 75/11 or 80/12 needle
- ruler
- marking pencil
- rotary cutter and mat (optional)
- craft knife
- scissors
- iron

Fabric

- 4 or 5 fat quarters
- one 12" x 15" (30.5 x 38 cm) piece of muslin

Other Supplies

- polyester or cotton thread
- 9" x 12" (23 x 30.5 cm) piece of foam board
- clear packing tape
- piece of yarn or string, for hanging (optional)

You already know

- How to use a rotary cutter and mat (page 124)
- How to sew a ¼" (6 mm) seam

You will learn

- The difference between pressing and ironing, and how to do each (page 126)
- How to make a base fabric

Directions

NOTES: Seam allowance: ¼" (6 mm)

Rotary cutters, craft knives, and irons should always be used with proper supervision.

1 Cut the fat quarters into 2" (5 cm) strips. You will be using all lengths of strips, but the longest needs to be at least 19" (48 cm).

2 Draw a 3¾" x 5¾" (9.5 x 14.5 cm) rectangle centered in the middle of your foam board. Using the craft knife, carefully cut out the rectangle to allow for photo placement later.

3 Center the foam board on the 12" x 15" (30.5 x 38 cm) piece of muslin and trace the inner and outer edges. This will be your guide for where the front of the frame will be.

4 Starting in one corner, place the first strip right side up on the diagonal (A). Lay your second strip butting up against the first strip, making sure you go from edge to edge of the muslin (B). (It is important to make sure your strips go from edge to edge of your muslin and not stop at the drawn outline so that you allow for the fabric to wrap around the edge of the foam board.) Flip the second strip over so it is right side down on top of the first strip. It helps if you can see a very little bit of the first fabric so that you know you will catch both pieces when you sew. Pin in place (C). These first two pieces (and the last two at the other corner) will not show very much on the final project, so don't use your favorite pieces!

5 Using a ¼" (6 mm) seam allowance, stitch two strips to the muslin, going from edge to edge of the muslin.

6 Flip the second strip right side up and press flat.

(continued)

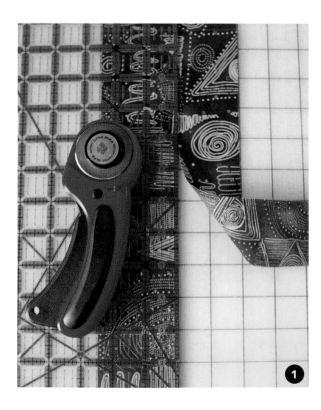

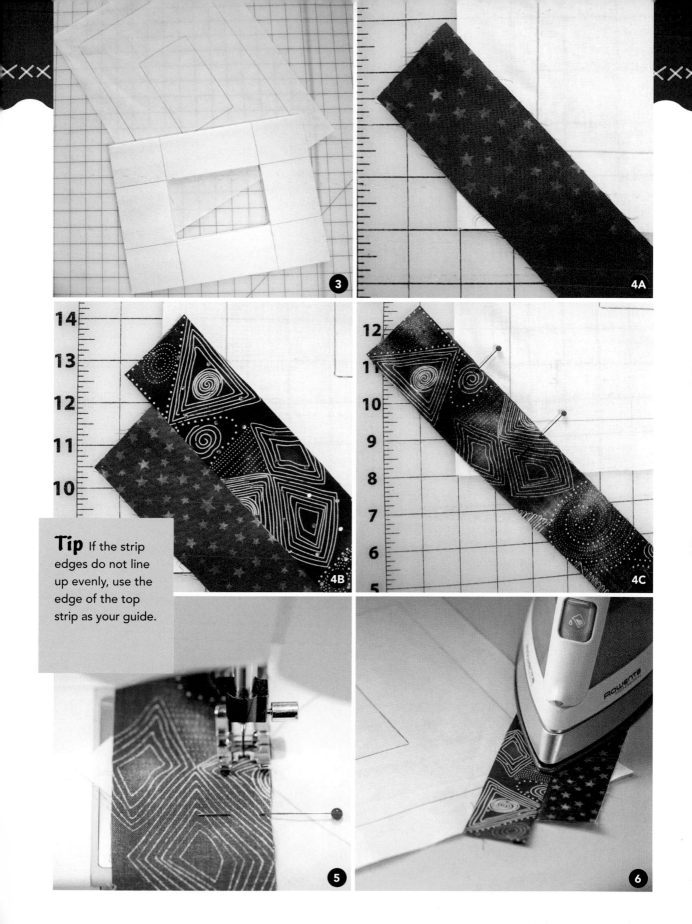

Tip If the strip edges do not line up evenly, use the edge of the top strip as your guide.

3

4A

4B

4C

5

6

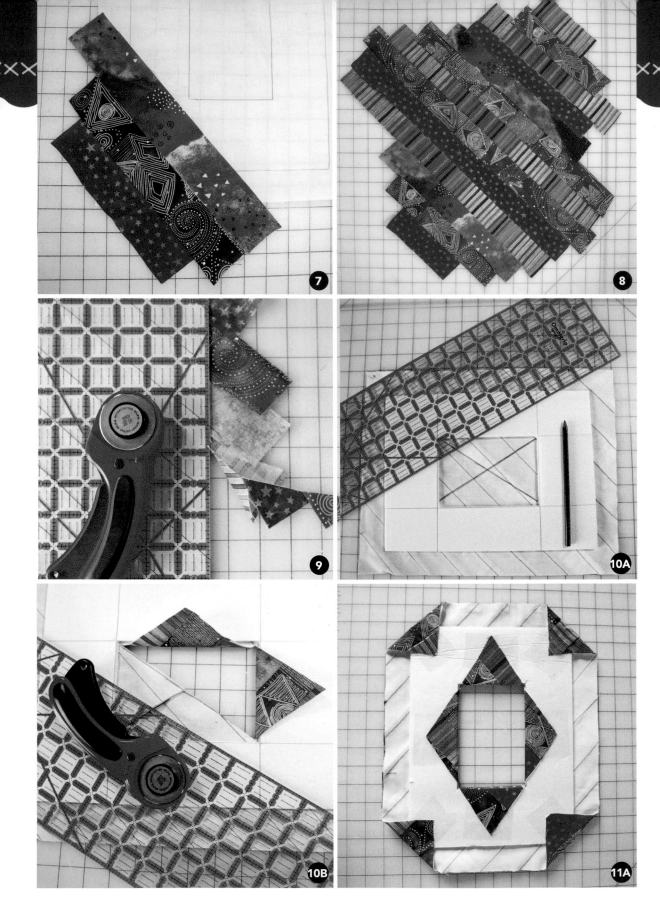

7   Add a third strip butting up to the second strip as before, again making sure the strip is long enough to go from edge to edge of the muslin. Flip the third strip onto the second and pin in place. Sew with ¼" (6 mm) seam allowance. Open and press flat.

8   Repeat step 7 until you have covered all of the muslin.

9   Turn the piece so that the muslin is showing. Using a ruler and a rotary cutter, trim the excess fabric along all four edges.

10 Place the foam board in the center of the muslin. Trace inside the rectangle and mark with an X (A). *Use the rotary cutter and ruler to cut along the lines of the X only*, leaving the flaps in place (B).

11 Place the foam board back onto the muslin and fold the inner flaps over, securing them with 2" (5 cm) pieces of packing tape (A). Fold the outer corners over and secure with 1½" (3.8 cm) pieces of packing tape. Cut two 11" (28 cm) pieces of tape and use to secure the folded-over long edges. Cut two 8" (20 cm) pieces of tape to secure the remaining short edges (B).

12 Tape a picture to the back of the frame so it shows through the center. If you would like to hang the frame, you can tape a loop of yarn or string to the back.

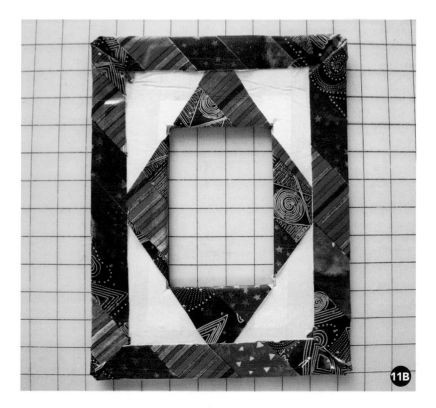

11B

1-1½
hours

Gift Giving Goodie Bag

Who can resist this fun, lined goodie bag? It's great for gift giving or just carrying around your stuff. Once you have mastered this project, make other bags in different sizes.

You will need

Tools

- size 80/12 needle
- pins
- hem gauge
- ruler
- tailor's chalk
- point turner
- iron
- sleeve board
- bodkin or safety pin

Fabric

- 2 fat quarters cotton fabric or ½ yd (0.5 m) each of two cotton fabrics

Other Supplies

- cotton/polyester thread
- ¾ yard (0.7 m) of ³⁄₈" (1 cm) to ⁵⁄₈" ribbon

You already know

- How to cut fabric
- How to sew a ³⁄₈" (1 cm) seam allowance
- How to pivot

You will learn

- How to use a hem gauge
- How to trim corners
- How to make a casing
- How to use a bodkin

Directions

NOTES: Seam allowance: 3/8" (1 cm)

In general, the inside lining fabric should be the same weight or lighter than the outside fabric.

1 Cut each fabric into one 15" x 20" (38 x 51 cm) piece. Place the fabric on the table with the right sides together and the 20" (51 cm) side along the top. Make sure the fabric you chose for the outside of the bag is on top. Pin along the top edge.

2 Stitch the seam using a 3/8" (1 cm) seam allowance (A). Stop and remove the pins as you come to them. Press the seam open (B).

3 In the upper right corner, use the hem gauge to measure down and mark lines at 2" and 2¾" (5 and 7 cm).

4 Fold the fabric right sides together lengthwise, matching the seams and raw edges (A). Pin the layers together along the three raw edges. Leave a 4" (10 cm) opening on the short edge of the lining and mark with double pins (B).

5 Using a hem gauge, mark a dot 3/8" (1 cm) from the edges at the two corners that don't have folds.

(continued)

> **Tips** Always stop stitching and remove pins as you come to them.

1

2A

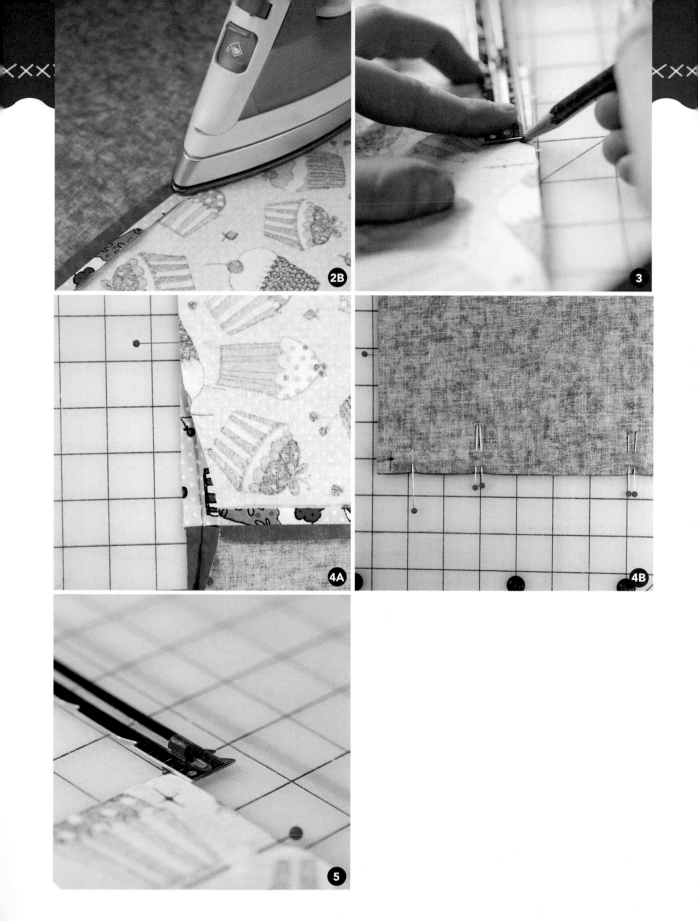

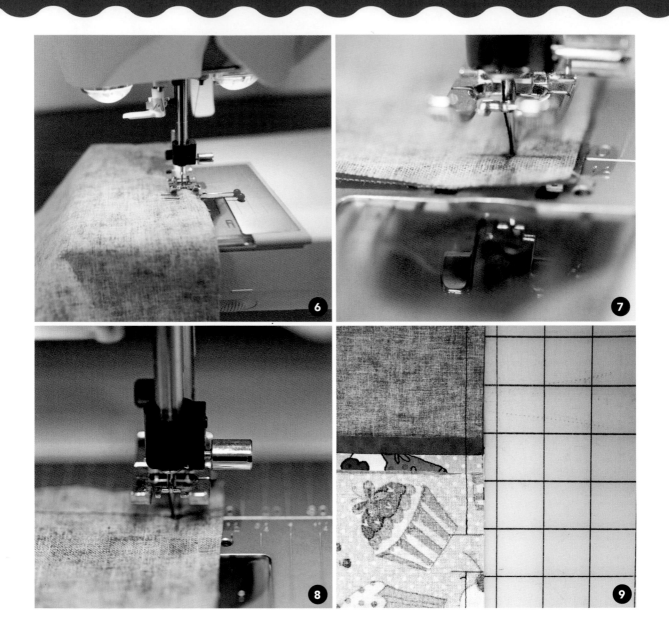

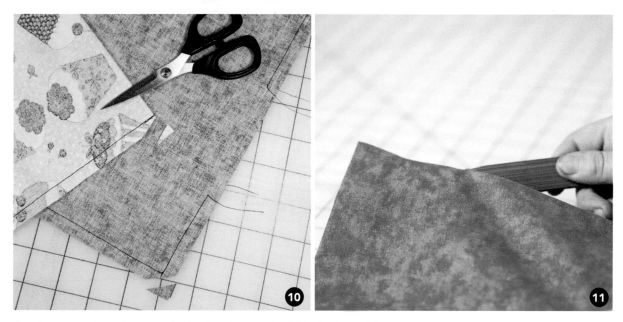

6 Begin stitching the seam by backtacking at the folded edge of the lining. Stitch up to the first double pin, stop, turn the handwheel until the needle and take-up lever are in the highest positions, lift the presser foot, and move the fabric to the next set of double pins, skipping the opening.

7 Lower the presser foot and continue to stitch until landing with the needle down on the corner dot. Turn the handwheel so the needle is all the way down in the fabric to anchor, then lift the presser foot.

8 Turn the fabric to pivot. Lower the presser foot. The fabric should now align to the 3/8" (1 cm) seam allowance again.

9 Stitch along the long edge until you get to the first marked line past the center seam. Backtack. Turn the handwheel until the needle and take-up lever are in the highest positions, and lift the presser foot to skip to just after the second line. Lower the presser foot and begin the seam again by backtacking to the second line, and then proceed to the corner dot. Pivot and stitch the last short edge and backtack at the fold.

10 Clip the threads in half at the openings, leaving tails. To reduce bulk in the corners, trim the seam allowance halfway to the stitches on all four corners.

11 Reach through the large opening in the lining and pull the fabric through to the right side. Use a point turner to poke the corners square, but be careful not to poke right through the fabric or the seam!

(continued)

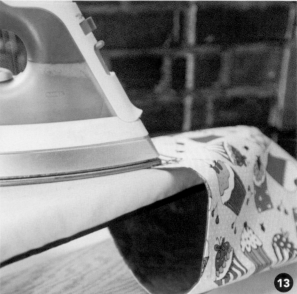

12 Press all the seams straight, making the bag flat. At the opening in the lining, tuck the seam allowance in even with the seam line and press flat. Pin the opening closed. Topstitch the opening closed by stitching close to the edge of the folds.

13 Tuck the lining into the bag, using your fingers to match the corners of the lining and the fabric. Slide the bag onto the sleeve board, and press the top edge so the seam is crisp and even.

14 Measure down from the top edge of the bag and draw a line at 2¾" (7 cm) and at 1¼" (3.2 cm) on both sides of the bag. These lines should line up to the opening in the side seam.

15 Pin the outer bag to the lining, pinning across the lines. Be careful not to catch the other side of the bag as you pin.

16 Remove the bed extension from the sewing machine to allow for sewing on the narrow free arm. Starting at the side seam, follow the line and stitch all around the bag. Repeat for the second line. This will form the casing for the ribbon.

17 Attach the bodkin to one end of the ribbon by closing the teeth to grip the end of the ribbon and sliding the ring on the bodkin down to hold it tightly closed. Thread the bodkin through the casing opening at the seam line (A). Scoot the bodkin all the way around the bag and out through the same hole. Remove the bodkin and pull the ribbon ends even. Tie a knot (B).

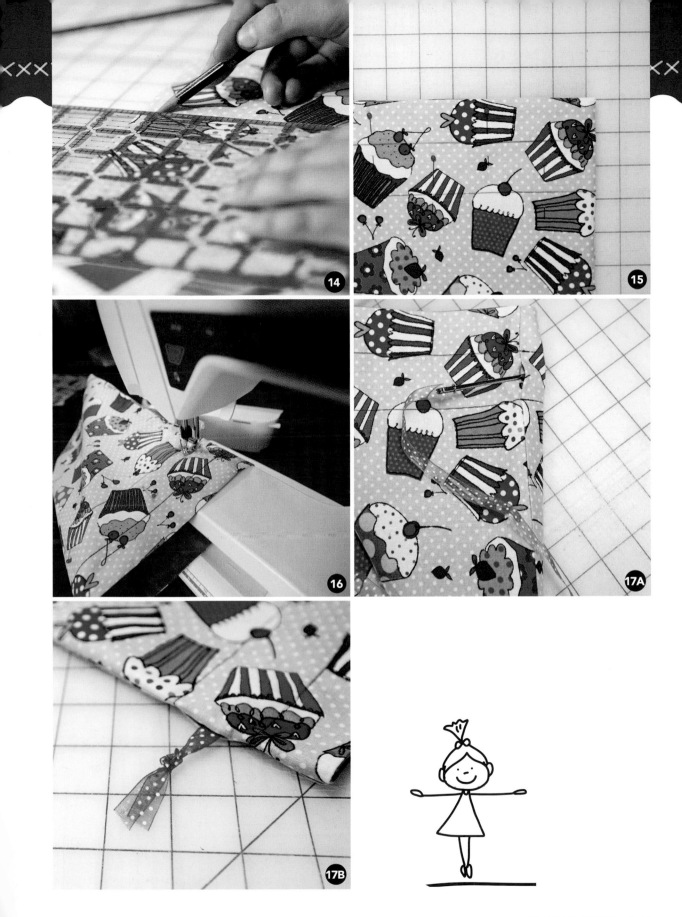

1-2 hours

Creative Cape

This colorful cape is reversible: one side is for creative embellishment and one side is for fun or fashion. Our teddy bear's cape has an S appliqué (for Sewing Superhero) applied over a star appliqué. Choose some fabulous fabric for a one-of-a-kind cape, be it for a superhero, a fashionista, or a furry friend!

You already know

- How to change your stitch
- How to change your stitch length/width
- How to use a bodkin (page 127)
- How to press
- How to mark an opening
- How to slipstitch by hand
- How to make a casing

You will learn

- How to pin for speed, accuracy, and ease of use
- How to make nice corners
- How to use a zigzag stitch
- How to use fusible web to attach an appliqué

You will need

Tools

- size 80/12 needle or appropriate for fabric chosen
- measuring tape
- scissors
- marking pencil
- iron and press cloth
- point turner
- bodkin or safety pin

Fabric

- 2 fat quarters or approximately ½ yard (45.5 cm) each of one plain and one print for front and back
- scrap fabric for appliqué

Other Supplies

- all-purpose thread
- ¼ yard (23 cm) paper-backed fusible web (Steam-A-Seam or Wonder-Under)
- 1 yard (1 m) ribbon or cording

Directions

NOTES: *Seam allowance: edge of your presser foot or ¼" (6 mm)*

You can use any fabric. If doing an appliqué, test the fabric for heat and fusing to make sure it does not melt.

1 Take the following measurements and write them down here or on a piece of paper.

  A Desired length: _____ + ½" (1.3 cm) = _____.

  B Desired collar height: _____

  C A + B = _____.

  D Width around at chest including arms: _____ x 1.5 for fullness = _____ + ½" (1.3 cm) = _____.

  Measurements A and D include ¼" (6 mm) seam allowances.

  Cut two cape pieces with length of C and width of D.

2 Design your appliqué and trace it onto the paper side of the fusible web. If it is a letter or number, it must be reversed (mirror image). Cut it out, leaving a small margin around the image. Place the design, fusible side down, on the wrong side of the appliqué fabric. Then fuse it in place following the fusible web manufacturer's instructions. Cut out the appliqué.

3 Peel the paper backing from the appliqué. Position the appliqué on the plain fabric, center horizontally and about one-third down from the upper edge. Fuse it in place, using a press cloth.

4 Zigzag stitch around the appliqué. Try to stitch so the right-hand stitch of the zigzag goes just over the outer edge of the appliqué. Stitch slowly to maneuver around curves. To pivot, stop with the needle down in the fabric in the right-hand stitch of the zigzag.

5 On the wrong side of one fabric, measure down from the upper edge a distance equal to the height of the collar (B) plus ¼" (6 mm) for the seam allowance, and draw a short line on the side seam allowance. Draw a second line 1" (2.5 cm) below the first line for the ribbon casing. Repeat on the opposite side seam allowance. Pin the right sides of the cape fabrics together, inserting the pins perpendicular to the raw edges with the heads on the outside. (This will make it easy to remove the pins as you sew.) Along the lower edge, leave an opening for turning the cape right side out, and double pin the starting and stopping points. Mark the pivot points ¼" (6 mm) in from all the corners.

6 Place the fabric under the presser foot just ahead of the double-pinned opening. Backtack. Stitch around the cape pivoting at the corners. Backtack above and below the casing lines on each side, creating the casing opening. Finish by backtacking on the opposite side of the opening.

7 Turn the cape right side out through the opening in the lower edge. Use a point turner to poke the corners square. Press the edges. Press under the seam allowances of the opening and pin them together. Slip stitch the opening closed (page 25).

8 Measure down from the upper edge of the cape to the height of the collar (B), and draw a line across the cape. Mark a second line 1" (2.5 cm) below the first line. Pin the layers together across the lines.

9 Stitch on the marked lines, backtacking at the beginning and end.

10 Attach the bodkin to one end of the ribbon. Thread the bodkin through one casing opening at the side seam. Draw the ribbon through the casing and out the other side.

11 Gather the cape onto the center of the ribbon to the desired fullness and comfort. Stitch across the ends of the casing to keep the ribbon in place.

Three Ways to Pin

- Pin perpendicular to the raw edges for easy removal of pins as you sew.
- Weave pins in and out at the stitching line.
- Pin away from the stitching line so you do not have to remove the pins as you sew.

Tip Use an iron with adult supervision.

2
hours

Keep It Close Bed Organizer

Struggling to find your book at night? Need a book light and don't want to get up? Have a thought and want to write it down before you forget? Make a fabulous bedside organizer and have everything at your fingertips! This project is easy to make and easy to modify to your specific needs. Use these techniques to design a locker organizer. Try an appliqué on the pockets!

You will need

Tools

- size 80/12 or 90/14 needle, depending on fabric choice
- ruler
- scissors
- rotary cutter and cutting mat (optional)
- pins
- hem gauge
- tailor's chalk or marking pencil
- point turner
- iron
- press cloth
- center guide foot for your machine (optional)
- Hump Jumper (optional)

Fabric

- ¾ yard (69 cm) each of 2 different corduroy or twill fabrics

Other Supplies

- cotton/polyester thread

Directions

NOTES: Seam allowances: ½" (1.3 cm) for body of organizer; ¼ (6 mm) for pockets

Choose a sturdy fabric for this to give it the body and strength it will need to hold up to use.

1 Cut one of each from *each* fabric.
Main piece:
20" x 36" (51 x 91 cm)
Pockets:
6½" x 5" (16.5 x 12.5 cm)
5" x 6½" (12.5 x 16.5 cm)
5" x 3" (12.5 x 7.5 cm)
4" x 5" (10 x 12.5 cm)

Tip Lay your fabrics right sides together and cut out fronts and back of organizer and pockets together. They will match better.

(continued)

You already know

- How to cut fabric
- How to pivot
- How to use a point turner
- How to close an opening
- How to trim corners

You will learn

- How to make a self-lined pocket
- How to topstitch

2   Lay the large pieces right sides together and pin around the four sides, leaving an 8" (20 cm) opening to turn.

3   Using a hem gauge, mark dots ½" (1.3 cm) from all four corners as a guide to where to pivot.

4   Start stitching at the double pin at the end of the opening, and stitch to the first corner. To pivot, lower the needle into the dot to anchor the fabric, and then lift the presser foot. Rotate the fabric to turn the corner, lining up the new edge with the ½" (1.3 cm) seam allowance, and lower the presser foot. Continue stitching to the next corner, where you will pivot and repeat until you end up at the beginning of your opening (double pin).

5   To reduce bulk, trim the corners halfway to the pivot point at each corner. This will allow the corners to lay flatter when turned. Reach your hand through the opening and pull the organizer through to turn it right side out.

6   Use a point turner to poke the corners square.

7   Press the seams and organizer flat. At the opening, tuck the seam allowance in and press flat to make a straight edge. Pin in place and stitch the opening closed, stitching close to the folded edge. This is called topstitching. Topstitch the other short end of the organizer a ¼" (6 mm) from the edge. Set aside for later.

8   To make each self-lined pocket, place the matching fabric pieces right sides together and pin around the edges, leaving an opening at the lower edge for turning. Double pin the opening. Just like you did for the body of the organizer, begin at the end of the opening and use a ¼" (6 mm) seam allowance to stitch all the way around pocket, pivoting at the corners and ending at the beginning of the opening. Trim the corners and turn right side out, using the point turner to square the corners. Press the pocket and opening flat (tucking the seam allowance in), but no need to stitch the opening closed. You will do this when you stitch it to the main body of the organizer. Topstitch ⅛" (3 mm) from the upper edge of each pocket. If you have a center guide foot, this is a good time to use it; move the needle over to the left position, and align the guide to the pocket edge.

9   Lay the organizer down with the wrong side facing up and the edge with the stitched opening along the top. Fold the bottom edge up 12" (30.5 cm) so that you can see the right side of the fabric. Mark the center seam line to divide the folded fabric into two pockets.

10 Lay the self-lined pockets on the organizer, placing them where you want but keeping them ¼ (6mm) away from the center line and 1" (2.5 cm) away from the sides, and with the openings at the bottom. Pin in place, being careful to pin only to the top folded piece of the main organizer, not pinning through to the back two layers.

11 Unfold the body of the organizer and topstitch each pocket in place ⅛" (3 mm) from the edge. Beginning at the upper edge, sew around the edge of the pocket, pivoting at the corners and backtacking at the beginning and end. Do not stitch the top of the pocket!

12 After all the pockets are secured, refold the main body 12" (30.5 cm) up so that the pockets are showing and pin the sides in place. Place pins horizontally across the line marking the center seam.

13 Topstitch two sides together from the top of the flap to the bottom using the edge of the presser foot as a guide. Backtack at beginning and end.

14 Beginning at the folded edge at the bottom of the organizer, stitch along the marked line to divide the body into two large pockets.

Tip
If you double pin the beginning and end of the opening, it will be easy to remember to not stitch there.

Tips Running your point turner along your seam lines from the inside will encourage your seams to lie flat, making it easier at the ironing board.

7

8

10

Tip You can also use a Hump Jumper (yellow tool in the photo) which will help you to stitch over the thick seams and folds.

11

12

13

1-1½
hours

Totally Cool Tool Carrier

This tool carrier is a fantastic way to stay organized! Store all your sewing tools in this pocketed carrier that rolls up and ties to keep them secure. This pattern can be adapted to store whatever you need. Try designing one for painting supplies, markers, crayons, or colored pencils. Recycle a pair of jeans for the denim, and add a pocket on the outside.

You will need

Tools

- size 90/14 needle
- ruler
- tailor's chalk, or marking pencil
- scissors or rotary cutter and mat
- pinking shears or pinking rotary cutter (optional)
- pins
- iron
- Hump Jumper (optional)

Fabric

- one 15" x 20" (38 x 51 cm) piece of denim
- ¾ yard (69 cm) of coordinating cotton fabric

Other Supplies

- all-purpose thread
- 52" (132 cm) of ¾" to 1" (2 to 2.5 cm)-wide ribbon

You already know

- The difference between pressing and ironing
- How to line up layers of fabric and pin carefully

You will learn

- How to mark stitch lines on top of fabric
- How to baste
- How to use a Hump Jumper (optional)
- How to fray fabric edges

12 Stitch the flap in place, using a ¼" (6 mm) seam allowance with no backtack. Remember: The edge of your presser foot is about 1/4" (6 mm) when your needle is in the center position. Use this as your guide to stitch across the fabric. Press the Top Flap toward the upper edge of the denim.

13 Measure up from the seam 2¼" (5.7 cm) and lightly draw a guide line across the Top Flap. Pin across the line to hold it in place. Mark a dot ½" (1.3 cm) in from the side on either end of the line. This is where you will begin and end your seam to allow the edges to fully fray. Beginning at the first dot, stitch along the line, ending at the dot on other end, backtacking at both the start and the end.

14 Fold the ribbon in half and pin the folded edge to the right side of the denim 1" (2.5 cm) up from the large pocket and 1" (2.5 cm) in from the edge (A). Baste in place (B). Starting at the bottom, stitch the side using ½" (1.3 cm) seam allowance.

When you reach the ribbon, stitch over it, backtack all the way across the ribbon, and stitch forward over it again to reinforce. Then continue stitching. Stop and backtack at the top stitching line. Take care not to catch the flap in the stitches (C). Repeat for the other side. Remove the basting stitch along the pocket edge.

15 Using ½" (1.3 cm) seam allowance, sew the sides of the flap, making sure to fold back the loose edge of denim so as not to catch it in the stitches.

16 Fray the edges if desired by pulling out one thread at a time.

17 Fill the pockets with your sewing tools. Fold the top flap down, roll up the carrier, and tie the ribbon. You're all set!

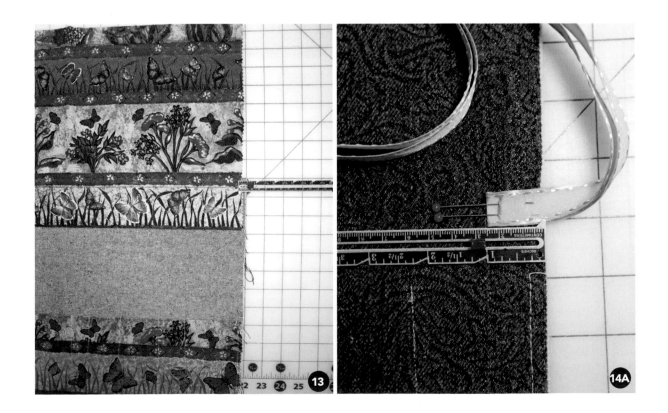

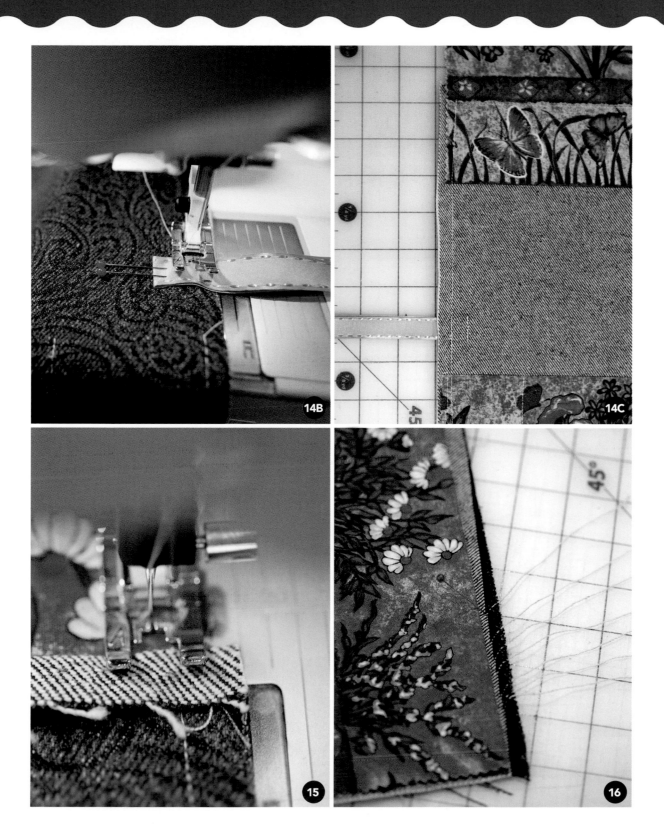

14B

14C

15

16

Crazy Quilt Bag

This bag is a great way to use up scrap fabrics from other projects. Add another pocket or zipper, two straps or one strap. You can try out your machine's decorative stitches or hand stitch embroidery stitches, too. Add beads, bangles, and buttons to personalize it and add some bling. This same method can be used to make fabric baskets or buckets in different sizes.

You will need

Tools

- size 80/12 needle
- scissors or rotary cutter and mat
- iron
- press cloth
- point turner
- tailor's chalk or pencil
- buttonhole foot if using a button for closure
- Fasturn for making stuffed tube handles or loop for button (optional)

Fabric

- one 12" x 18" (30.5 x 45.7 cm) piece of muslin or base fabric
- one 12" x 18" (30.5 x 45.7 cm) piece of fusible craft fleece or flannel
- one 12" x 18" (30.5 x 45.7 cm) piece of lining fabric
- variety of fabric scraps for piecing
- two 5" x 7" (12.5 x 17.8 cm) pieces of lining fabric or fun fabric for pockets
- two 18" x 4" (45.7 x 10 cm) strips of fabric for straps
- two 18" x 1" (45.7 x 2.5 cm) strips of fusible craft fleece or flannel

Other Supplies

- all-purpose thread
- contrasting or decorative thread
- button and ribbon for closure (optional)

You already know

- How to sew ¼" (6 mm) and ½" (1.3 cm) seams
- How to cut fabric
- How to topstitch
- How to make a self-lined pocket

You will learn

- How to crazy quilt
- How to make straps
- How to create a lining with fusible backing
- How to use a base fabric
- How to use decorative stitches
- How to make corners at the bottom of a bag

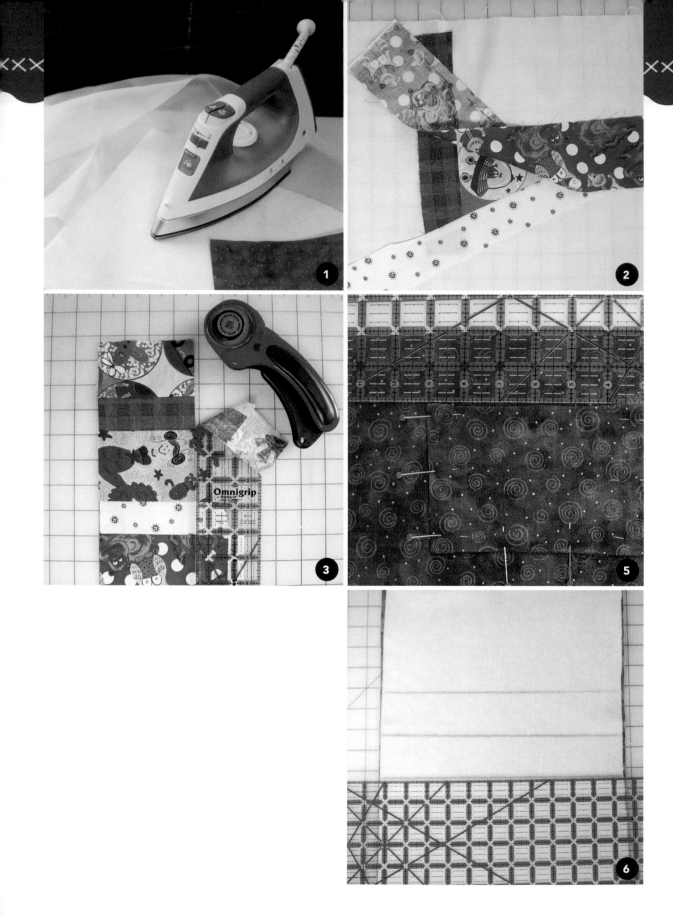

Directions

NOTES: Seam allowance: ¼" (6 mm) or edge of presser foot makes it easy for piecing. For exact ¼" (6 mm), use a quilting/piecing ¼" (6 mm) foot for sewing the strips together. Use a ½" (1.3 cm) seam allowance for construction of the lining and the bag.

1 With an iron and press cloth, press the fusible fleece to the lining to fuse in place.

2 From piecing scraps cut a triangle and place on the bottom or middle section of the muslin/base fabric. Cut the other fabrics into strips of different widths. Place one strip, right side down, along an edge of the triangle. Stitch ¼" (6 mm) from the edges, stopping just past the triangle point. Trim off the extra length from the strip, and press the strip away from the triangle. Place another strip face down on the next side of the triangle, also covering the previous strip. Stitch, trim, and press the strip away from the triangle. Repeat on the last side of the triangle, this time covering both previous strips with the new strip.

3 Create pieced strips by sewing several small pieces together and then trimming them to even up the edges.

4 Continue to add piecing scraps to the raw edges of previous strips until the entire muslin is covered. Turn the muslin over and trim off any extending fabric pieces. Baste around the edges to secure.

5 Place the two pocket pieces right sides together and stitch around, leaving an opening for turning. Clip the corners to reduce bulk. Turn the pocket right side out. Push out the corners using a point turner. Center the pocket on the lining/fleece piece 2" (5 cm) down from the top, and sew the pocket to the lining along the sides and bottom.

6 Draw a line across the middle of the fleece/lining and 1½" (3.8 cm) above and below that line using chalk or pencil.

7 Fold the lining in half right sides together. Sew up the side seams with a ½" (1.3 cm) seam allowance, backtacking at the beginning and end.

(continued)

> **Tips** When adding scraps or strips, extend them past the piece you are stitching to.

8 To make square corners, flatten one corner into a triangle with the seam going down the center. The sides of the triangle should intersect the two marked lines on the bag bottom. Draw a line across the bottom of the triangle where the lines intersect. Stitch across the corner (A). Trim off the triangle about ⅜" (1 cm) from the stitching line (B). Repeat on the other corner.

9 Repeat steps 5 to 7 with the outer bag piece.

10 To make the straps, press the 18" x 4" (45.7 x 10 cm) strap pieces in half lengthwise (wrong sides together). Unfold. Refold one long edge in to the center fold; press. Repeat on the other side. Unfold the strap and insert a fleece strip into it. Refold along the pressed lines encasing the fleece, and pin in place. Stitch close to both outside edges. Then stitch two more rows evenly spaced between them.

11 Slip the lining into the outer bag (A). Fold down the upper edge of the lining ½" (1.3 cm) and pin. Then fold down the upper edge of the outer bag and pin it to the lining, matching the upper folds and the side seams. Position the straps where you want them with the ends between the lining and outer bag; pin. If you want a button and ribbon loop, determine how long the loops should be and pin the ends between the bag layers (B).

12 Topstitch ¼" (6 mm) from the upper edge, catching the straps and ribbon loop in the stitching. For extra strength, you can stitch a second line.

13 Sew on the button so the ribbon can loop around it securely without bunching.

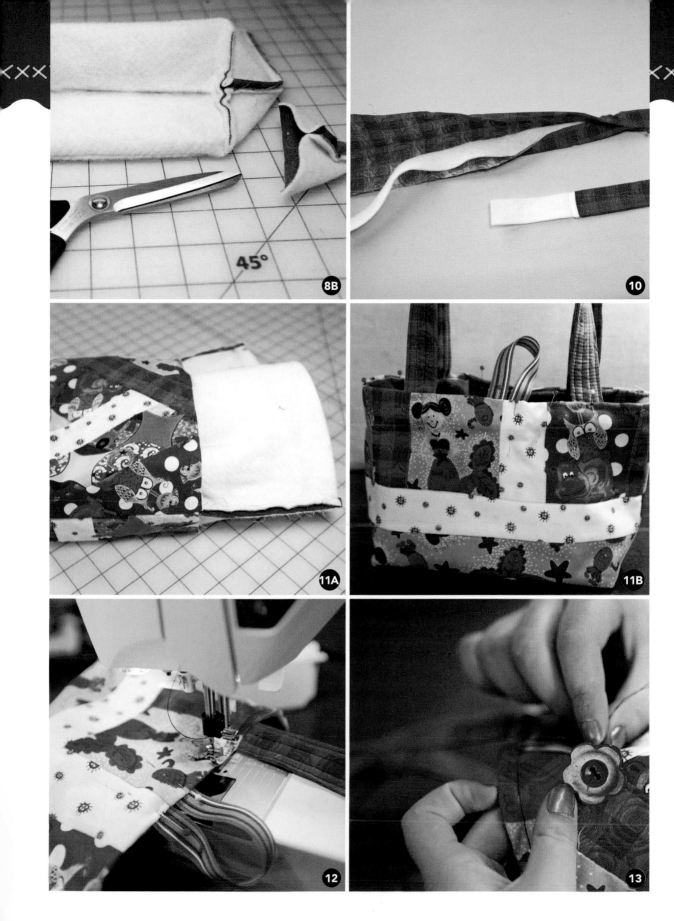

Secret Pocket Pillow

It's a pillow with a secret zipper pocket. Or it's a messenger bag or laptop bag with a zipper pocket—just add a strap. There are many ways to personalize it: add a big button for a closure, add some appliqués, or sew fringe around the flap.

You will need

Tools

- size 80/12 needle for cotton or one appropriate for your choice of fabric
- measuring tape
- scissors or rotary cutter and mat
- old scissors for cutting zipper
- marking pencil
- pins
- point turner
- iron and press cloth

Fabric

- 1 yard (91 cm) of 45" (114 cm)-wide main fabric (extra fabric for a large or repeat design)
- ½ yard (46 cm) of contrasting fabric for flap
- ½ yard (46 cm) of coordinating fabric or muslin for interior pocket

Other Supplies

- all-purpose thread
- 12" x 18" (30.5 x 46 cm) pillow form
- 14" (35.5 cm) zipper in a matching color
- scrap of fusible interfacing
- button for closure on flap

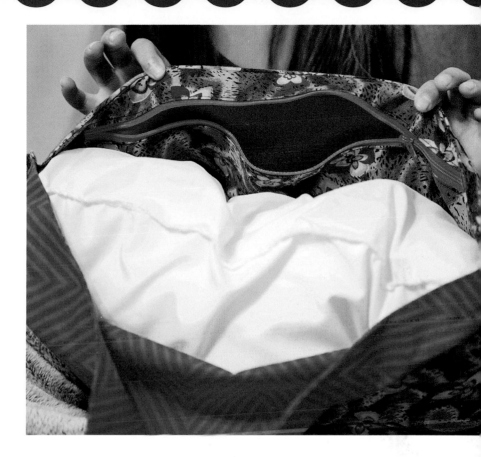

You already know

- How to measure and cut
- How to stitch and pivot
- How to trim corners
- How to topstitch
- How to sew on a button

You will learn

- How to insert a welt pocket zipper
- How to use fusible interfacing to stabilize a buttonhole

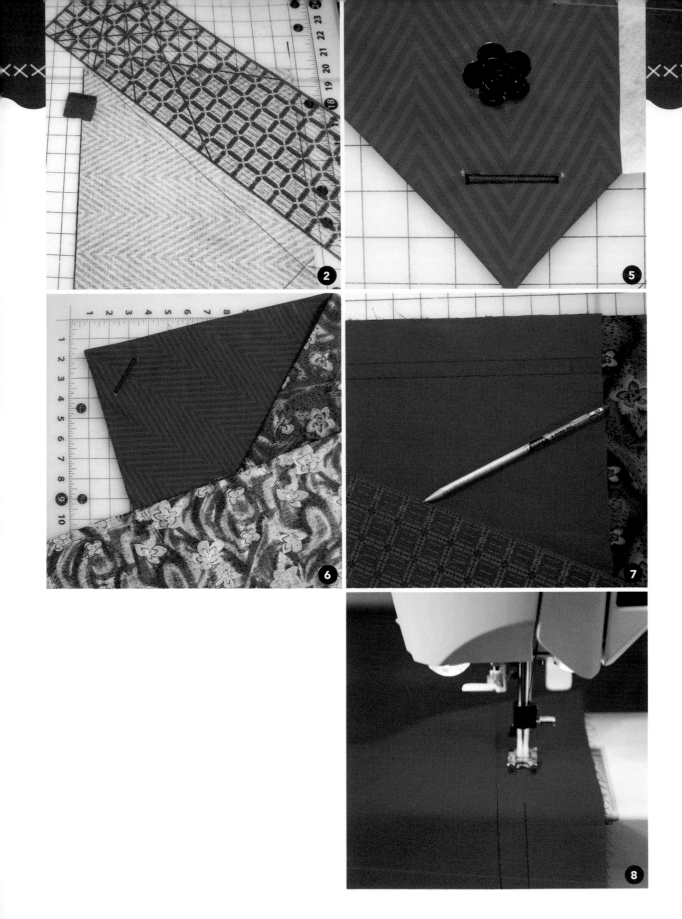

Directions

NOTES: Seam allowance: ½" (1.3 cm)

Launder your fabric to preshrink it.

1 Cut the following pieces:
four 14" x 20" (35.6 x 51 cm) pieces from main fabric
two 11" x 20" (28 x 51 cm) pieces from flap fabric (you design how much flap you want and the shape of the flap)
two 10" x 16" (25.5 x 40.5 cm) pieces from pocket fabric

2 To make a triangle flap, place the two flap fabric pieces right sides together. Mark the center of the 20" (51 cm) side ½" (1.3 cm) from the edge. Draw a line from both top corners through the ½" (1.3 cm) mark.

Note

You can design another shape for the flap—curved or straight—if you prefer.

3 Pin along the triangle sides and stitch, leaving the upper edge open and backtacking at the beginning and end. Pivot at the point.

4 Cut ½" (1.3 cm) from the stitching line and trim the point to reduce bulk. Iron a patch of fusible interfacing in the area of the point where you want a buttonhole. Turn right side out through the opening, push out the corners with a point turner, and press.

5 Mark a line where you want the buttonhole. It should be slightly longer than the button diameter. To make a buttonhole in the flap, see your machine for instructions.

6 Place two pillow rectangles right sides together with the triangle sandwiched between them on the wide top edge. Pin the edges, leaving about a 5" (12.5 cm) opening for turning. Stitch around the perimeter, using a ½" (1.3 cm) seam allowance. Clip the corners, turn right side out, push out the corners with a point turner, and press.

7 On one of the remaining two pillow rectangles, place one of the pocket rectangles right sides together and centered along a wide edge. Mark a line along the pocket 1½" (3.8 cm) from the top edge. Draw another line ½" (1.3 cm) below. Mark 1" (2.5 cm) in from each side.

8 Stitch the rectangle, starting in the center of the long line, and reduce the stitch length ½" (1.3 cm) from corner, pivot, stitch to the next corner, pivot, stitch ½" (1.3 cm) then return to the regular stitch length and continue. Reduce stitch length and pivot at the opposite end; then finish stitching the rectangle.

(continued)

9 Cut along the center of the rectangle to within ½" (1.3 cm) of the ends. Clip to the corners, being careful not to clip into the stitches.

10 Pull the pocket out through the opening and press. This will be the zipper opening.

11 Place the zipper underneath, showing through the opening, and pin. With the foot edge aligned against the zipper teeth, topstitch around, stitching close to the edge of the opening, and pivoting at the corners. Carefully walk your needle over the zipper at the ends.

12 Pin the two pocket pieces together and stitch around all four sides. Do not stitch onto the pillow piece.

13 Pin the other pillow piece right sides together to the rectangle with the pocket and stitch around, leaving an opening along the bottom for turning. Trim the corners, turn right side out, push out the corners with a point turner, and press.

14 Pin the two pillow pieces together on the sides and bottom, with the secret pocket on the inside and the triangle flap extending up. Topstitch the three sides, guiding the edge of the presser foot along the pillow edges, being careful to stitch the opening closed at the bottom.

15 Mark the placement for the button and sew it on.

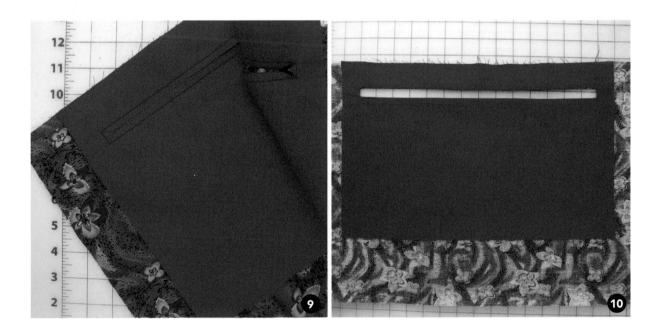

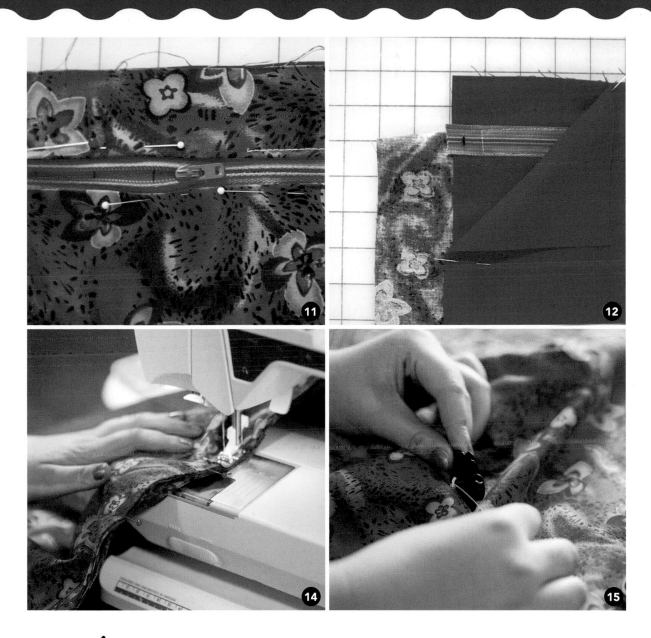

2-3
hours

Fish Coin Purse

This fish coin purse will have you swimming with embellishment opportunities! Our original fish includes decorative stitching, topstitching on the tail, hand beading for the eye, and a cool zipper insertion. You will also learn how to sew curves and how to use fusible interfacing to make the fish keep its shape.You can use metallic thread to topstitch, hand bead scales on the fish body, or use plain fabric and decorative stitches to create scales. Once you master this fish purse, try changing the shape of the purse by drawing your own simple shape on paper and use that as your pattern. You will still need to cut two of them out along with the interfacing and then use the directions to complete your original coin purse.

You will need

Tools

- size 80/12 needle
- marking pencil
- scissors
- iron
- 2 press cloths
- pins
- point turner
- hand needle for beading
- old pair of scissors for zipper
- seam ripper

Fabric

- two 10" x 7" (25.5 x 18 cm) pieces of cotton fabric for body
- two 7" x 5" (18 x 12.5 cm) pieces of cotton fabric for tail
- ¼ yard (23 cm) craft-weight fusible interfacing

Other Supplies

- all-purpose thread
- 9" (23 cm) zipper
- 7" (18 cm) of ½" (1.3 cm)-wide grosgrain ribbon
- rayon or metallic decorative thread
- beads for eye

Patterns

- fish body
- fish tail

You already know

- How to topstitch
- How to transfer markings from a pattern

You will learn

- How to use fusible interfacing
- How to trim curves
- How to do an exterior zipper insertion
- How to bead by hand

10 Pin and baste the tail to the right side of the zipper side of the body, using the placement lines.

11 With a hand needle, sew a bead for the eye on the zipper side of the body at the dot. Top a large with a smaller bead. Thread a needle with double thread and tie a knot in the end. Come up from the back of the fabric through the large bead and the small bead. Then run the needle back down through the large bead only, and tie off the thread on the back. Fold the ribbon in half and pin the ends to the zipper side of the body at the top. Baste ¼" (6 mm) from the edges. (Remember, when you baste, lengthen the stitch length. A baste is used to temporarily hold something in place and is usually stitched within your final seam allowance.)

12 Open the zipper halfway to allow for turning later. Match the body pieces right sides together and pin. Using a ⅜" (1 cm) seam allowance, begin stitching just before ribbon and continue all around the fish body, going over the ribbon again; backtack over the ribbon to reinforce the handle.

13 Trim the seam allowance to within ⅛" (3 mm) of the stitching line to allow the curves to relax. Because the body of the fish is fused to craft-weight interfacing, you can trim close without fear of fraying. Use your oldest pair of scissors to trim the zipper to avoid damaging good shears.

14 To expose the zipper, cut the fabric in between the decorative stitch lines through one layer of fabric. You can use a seam ripper to get the cutting line started.

15 Turn the purse right side out and use the point turner to smooth out the curves. Press flat using a press cloth to protect the zipper teeth, being careful not to put the iron on the zipper head. Fold the tail flat and press.

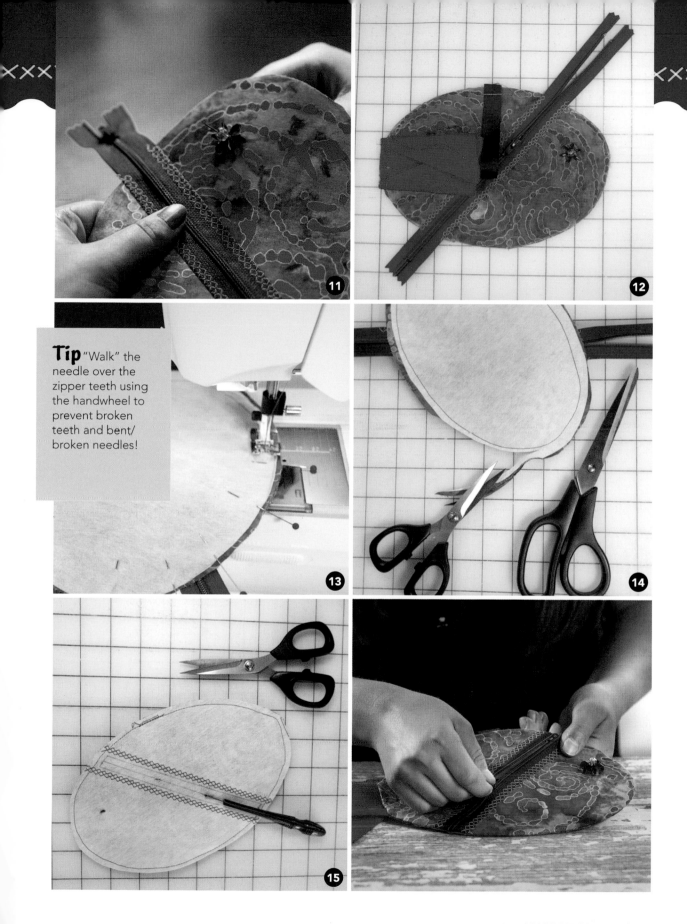

Tip "Walk" the needle over the zipper teeth using the handwheel to prevent broken teeth and bent/broken needles!

Creative Design

Whatever your interest in sewing or your skill level or sewing knowledge, sewing offers unlimited opportunities for creative fun. Garment sewing is the ultimate—sew it, wear it, and show off your skill, artistry, and fashion sense. Sewing is a skill that grows with every project. If you enjoy sewing, there are exciting careers in fashion, textiles, writing, art, publications—the list goes on.

Some Basics about Sewing Garments

 This chapter explores three garment projects that use your measurements to create the pattern. Yes, it is math and geometry. Basic garments move into more complicated and exciting garments as your skills, knowledge, and fearlessness grow. More complicated garments take longer, but they also offer more opportunity to learn. Don't worry about making a mistake: mistakes offer the best opportunity to problem solve, experiment, and develop confidence and skill. Once you have explored the relationship of your measurements to your finished garment, you are ready to interpret commercial patterns and move on to the exciting world of garment construction and design.

The fabric you choose is important. When you are testing a pattern it is helpful to make a "muslin." This is a test garment to see whether you like the way it feels and fits, and it gives you a chance to make changes—should it be longer or shorter, wider or slimmer?

Preparing the fabric is essential, because you need to plan how you will launder the piece once it is finished. Some fabrics shrink, so pre-washing and drying are musts—you wouldn't want your garment to shrink and become too small to wear after all your hard work! Using an iron for pressing is as essential as the sewing machine.

Edge finishing is important, too. You certainly don't want fraying threads everywhere. Each of our garments offers different edge finishing methods. The shorts have a "ready to wear" edge finishing that is stitched after the seam is created. The poncho requires no edge finishing because the fabric used does not ravel, and the kimono has French (or enclosed) seam edges.

For tools, you'll definitely need a flexible measuring tape. Also helpful are a French curve, a design ruler, and a seam allowance curve (or you can use a plate to draw the curve).

Tips for Success

- Measure accurately and record your measurements.

- Choose a quality fabric and preshrink it following the manufacturer's instructions printed on the bolt.

- Don't skip important steps like staystitching a neck curve, clipping into a seam to release the strain in the seam allowance, or notching a curve to allow it to lie flat.

- Press carefully and often.

- When stitching, keep the garment to the left of the needle (don't sew with the bulk inside the keyhole).

- Insert pins perpendicular to the seam, with the heads near the cut edges. This will make the pins easy to remove as you sew. Do not sew over pins (if the needle hits the pin, it will break the needle).

- If your stitches are crooked, then you will need to take them out by using a seam ripper. A crooked seam will show. Lay your seam ripper down flat and slip it under the stitch to slice the thread. Cut every three to five stitches and then take the thread from the other side and pull.

- Stitch the seam and then edge finish both together. Or edge finish all vertical edges before you stitch the seams.

- Press as you sew: after you have stitched a few seams, take the time to press the seams. This will give your garment a more polished, professional look. Make sure you test a scrap of fabric and adjust your heat setting if needed. Press the stitch line, then press the seam allowances open or to one side depending on your seam finishing decision. Press in the direction you sew.

- Notches on pattern cutting lines are shaped like diamonds and these symbols will be matched up when stitching one piece to another. Cut the diamonds out into the fabric, not into the garment seam.

- You can also mark notches using dressmaker's chalk, which brushes off.

- There are single, double, and triple notches. Sew the single notch seams first, and then sew the double notch seams.

- When cutting, go slowly. Place your free hand on the fabric and pattern to keep it flat and stable. Cut with long, even strokes (open your scissors up as far as possible for a long, even cut). Keep the pattern pieces with the cut fabric in case you need to refer back to them.

- Mark cut pieces with chalk on the wrong side of the fabric (an "F" for front and a "B" for back) to help you remember what they are.

1-2
hours

Shorts

You are going to make a pattern based on your measurements. It is a good idea to make a test garment first before making your favorite fabric into a garment to make sure your pattern will work for you. A test garment also helps you decide on embellishments (trims and cool stuff) and pockets and is a great way to practice hemming techniques and pocket placement. This pattern will be great for costumes, too. To spice things up, add rickrack or ribbon. Use a double needle or special thread and add decorative stitches. You can choose how full to make the bottom of your shorts/pants. For yoga pants, keep them full at the bottom.

You already know

- How to straight stitch
- How to backtack
- How to topstitch
- How to transfer markings
- How to make a casing for elastic
- How to use a bodkin

You will learn

- How to make a pattern using your body measurements
- How to add garment ease (enough room, or fullness, to get pants on and off and to sit down)
- How to edge finish a raw edge to avoid fraying
- How to hem shorts
- How to use notches
- How to work with straight of grain and why it is important

Directions

NOTES: If you want your shorts to sit on your hip bones, not at your natural waist, don't try to figure that into the measurements now. You can make that adjustment just before sewing the elastic casing in step 10.
Seam allowance: ⅝" (1.6 cm)

Stitch length: 2.5 or 10 to 12 stitches per inch (2.5 cm)

The pattern for the shorts has no side seams. It includes one-half of the front and back, the center front seam which continues into the crotch, center back seam which continues into the crotch, and the inseam (inner leg).

1 Take the following measurements using a flexible measuring tape:

   Hip measurement = _____

   Add 7" (17.8 cm) = _____ (ease and seam allowances)

   Divide by 2 = _____ (half-hip pattern measurement)

   Sit on a chair. Measure from your natural waist to the chair seat. This is your crotch length. = _____

   Length from natural waist to knee (or desired length) = _____

2 Now it is time to draw your pattern. You will need a piece of paper longer than your garment and wider than your half hip measurement. We used a piece of paper 30" (76 cm) wide and 28" (71 cm) long for shorts on page 94.

Marks on the Grainline

A Draw a line down the middle of the paper from top to bottom. This is the straight of grain line.

B Draw a mark on the grainline from the top of the paper down 2½" (6.4 cm) for the waistline. This will allow for a casing for elastic that is ¾" (2 cm) wide.

C Draw a mark on the grainline from the waistline mark down to the crotch length.

D Draw a mark from the crotch length up 3½" (8.9 cm) for the hip.

E Draw a mark from the waistline to the desired length.

F Draw a mark from the length down 1½" (3.8 cm) for the hem.

Horizontal Lines

Note:
Draw these lines perpendicular to the straight grainline.

G Draw a line equal to your half hip measurement at the hip mark, waistline mark, crotch mark, and hem mark. These lines should extend equally to both sides.

H Extend the crotch, finished length, and hem lines 3" (7.5 cm) to the right (this is the front of the shorts).

I Extend the crotch, finished length, and hem lines 4½" (11.4 cm) to the left (this is the back of the shorts).

J Using a curve (or a round saucer or plate) connect end of the hip line to the end of the crotch line on front and back.

Vertical Lines (sides)

K Connect the marks on both sides of the pattern from the top of the waist to the hip. These are the center front and center back seamlines.

L Connect the marks on both sides of the pattern from the crotch to the hem. These are the inseam seamlines.

Finishing Marks

M On the left side write "back" and on the right side write "front."

N From the crotch line, go down 3" (7.5 cm) and make a single notch on both the front and back inseam seamlines.

O From the waistline, measure down 3" (7.5 cm) along center front line and make a double notch.

P From the waistline, measure down 3" (7.5 cm) along the center back line and make a triple notch.

(continued)

> **Tip** Your natural waist is the smallest part, and the hip measurement is the biggest part.
>
> Don't skip steps N, O, and P. Those notches are important!

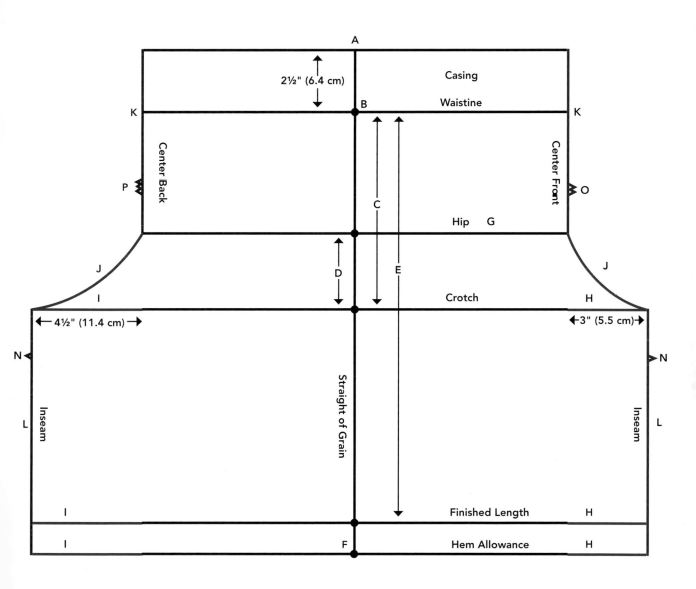

A

2½" (6.4 cm)

Casing

B   Waistline

K   K

Center Back

P

C

Center Front

O

Hip   G

D

J   J

I   Crotch   H

4½" (11.4 cm)   3" (5.5 cm)

N   N

E

Inseam   Straight of Grain   Inseam

L   L

I   Finished Length   H

I   F   Hem Allowance   H

3 Lay the fabric on the table, folded in half length-wise, right sides together, with selvages even. Place your pattern on your fabric so the grainline runs parallel to the selvages. Use pattern weights to hold the pattern in place (as shown) or pin the pattern to the fabric.

4 Cut out your fabric. You will have two identical pieces, one for the left front/back and one for the right front/back. Before removing the pattern from the fabric, transfer the notch marks from the pattern to the fabric.

5 Fold one piece in half, right sides together. Pin the inseams together, matching the notches. Repeat for the other piece.

6 Stitch with a ⅝" (1.6 cm) seam allowance, back-tacking at the beginning and end of each seam. Using a zigzag stitch or an overcast foot and overcast stitch, finish the seam allowances of one inseam together. Repeat for the other inseam.

7 Press one inseam toward the front of the shorts. Press the other inseam toward the back of the shorts.

8 Turn one leg right side out and leave the other wrong side out. Insert the right-side-out leg into the wrong-side-out leg. Pin the center front, crotch, and center back seam, matching the in-seams and keeping the seam allowances turned in the direction they were pressed.

9 Stitch the seam in one continuous stitching line, backtacking at the beginning and end. Stitch a second time just to the outside of the first stitching line in the area of the crotch. Edge-finish the seam allowances together as you did for the inseams. Press them to one side.

Note
Here is where you can change where the top of your shorts rests. Try the shorts on, and tie or pin a length of ¾" (2 cm) elastic around the top where you would like the shorts to rest. Make sure the crotch length feels comfortable and the fabric extends above the elastic the same amount all around. Mark where the top of the elastic sits with a safety pin at the front seam, and remove the shorts. Measure up 1¾" (4.5 cm) above the safety pin and mark. Measure from this mark to the upper edge of the shorts, and trim off this amount evenly all the way around.

10 Stitch the top 1¾" (4.5 cm) of the center back seam allowance to the garment. This will help you slide the elastic through the casing without getting stuck on the seam allowance.

11 To create the waistline casing for the elastic, press the top under ¼" (6 mm). Then press it under again 1½" (1.3 cm). Pin it in place, leaving an opening across the center back seam for inserting the elastic. Place two pins at the stitch starting point and two pins at the stopping point. Stitch along the inner fold starting and stopping at the double pins.

12 Measure your waist and subtract 3" (7.5 cm) for the length of the elastic, or just try it around your waist and cut it to a comfortable length. Insert the elastic into the casing using a bodkin or safety pin.

13 Pull out the ends of the elastic and make sure the elastic is not twisted. Abut the ends of the elastic, and wrap them with a small piece of fabric (A). Zigzag back and forth across both ends through the fabric (B). Trim away excess fabric.

14 Ease the elastic back into the casing. Sew the opening of the casing closed.

15 To hem, fold the bottom up ¼" (6 mm) and press. Then turn it up again 1¼" (3.2 cm) and press. Make sure the seam allowance goes in the same direction as it was pressed. Pin in place. Stitch close to the inner fold.

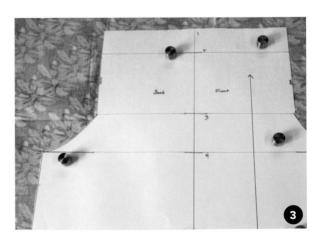

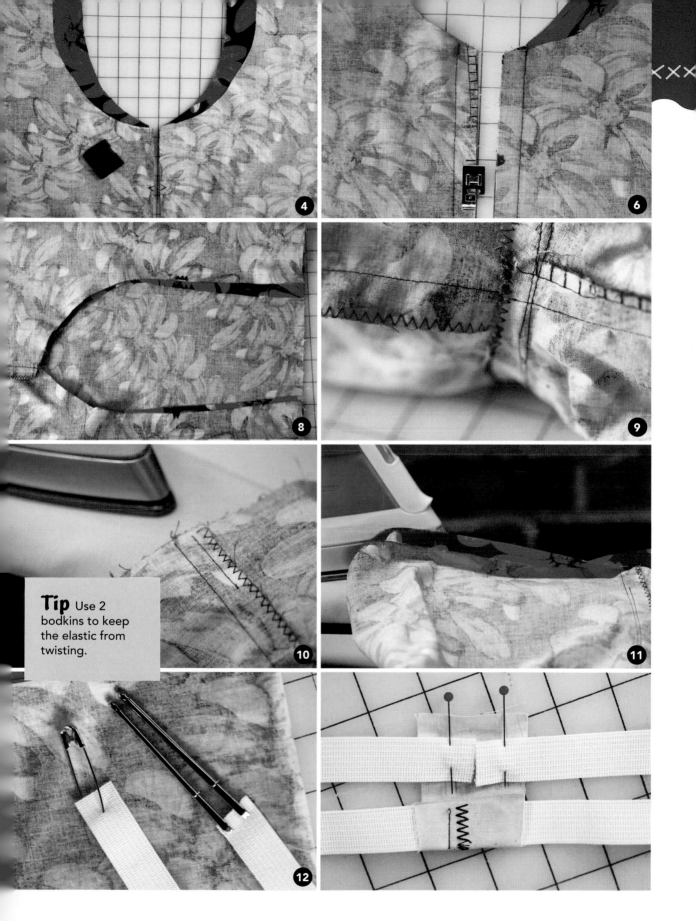

Tip Use 2 bodkins to keep the elastic from twisting.

2-3
hours

Kimono

This versatile and easy kimono-style garment can be adapted and embellished. Make it long or short, curved or straight, fancy or let the fabric speak for itself. Once you've learned the ropes, have fun creating a robe, a blouse, a jacket, a coat, or a beach cover-up. Add pockets, choose a different fabric for the band and belt, or design larger sleeves for a more dramatic costume look. French seams beautifully finish off your garment, but if you have less time you can finish the seams the usual way.

You already know

- How to backtack
- How to measure your body
- How to make a pattern
- How to sew a topstitch hem
- How to machine stitch and follow a seam allowance

You will learn

- How to make a French seam which beautifully finishes off your interior seams
- How to make a belt and belt loops
- How to make a pocket
- How to make a band

You will need

Tools

- size 80/12 needle or one appropriate for your choice of fabric
- flexible measuring tape
- scissors or rotary cutter and mat
- tailor's chalk or marking tool
- seam allowance curve ruler, French curve, or design ruler

Fabric

- 2 yards (183 cm) of 45" (114 cm)-wide fabric for a knee-length garment or 3 yards (274 cm) of 45" (114 cm)-wide fabric for an ankle-length garment

Other Supplies

- all-purpose polyester thread

Directions

NOTES: Seam allowance: ¼" (6 mm), ⅜" (1 cm), and ⅝" (1.6 cm)

If you choose a fabric that will fray easily, edge finish before construction. The directions include how to make French seams.

Our calculations are for a knee-length garment in a child's size 8, with a neck-to-waist length of 12" (30.5 cm) and a shoulder width of 12" (30.5 cm). For adult sizes, the fabric width may necessitate creating a shoulder seam and folding the fabric lengthwise to cut the back and front separately.

1 These directions will show you how to figure out the measurements for any size. The examples in bold are for a child's size 8 (see Notes).

Shoulder to knee for length of garment = **32" (81.3 cm)** (adjust for ankle-length)_____

Add 2" (5 cm) for hem = **34" (86.4 cm)** _____

Double (x 2) for front and back = **68" (172.7 cm)** _____(A)

Neck to natural waist for back length = **12" (30.5 cm)** _____

Around chest, including arms = **25" (63.5 cm)** _____

Add 2" (5 cm) for ease to get back width = **27" (68.6 cm)** _____(B)

Divide by 2 for each front width = **13½" (34.3 cm)** each side of the front _____(C)

Shoulder width = **12" (30.5 cm)** _____

Subtract 2" (5 cm) for sleeve length = **10" (25.5 cm)** _____(D)

Add shoulder width **(12" [30.5 cm])** and ½ back length **(6" [15 cm])** for sleeve width = **18" (45.7 cm)** _____(E)

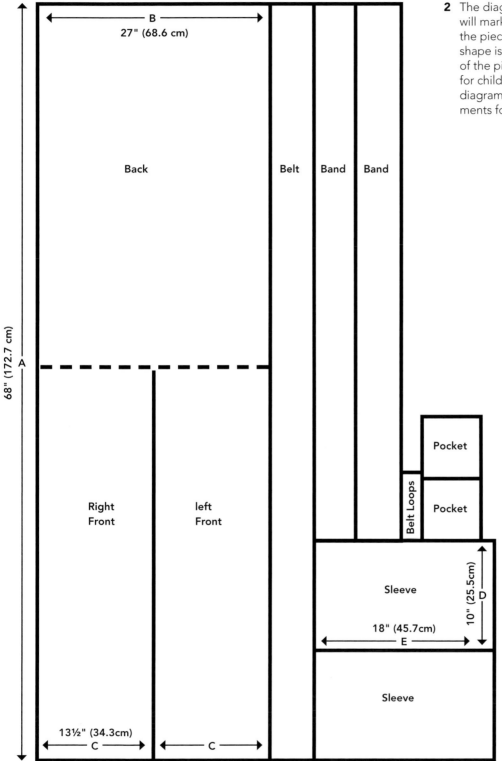

2 The diagram shows how you will mark the fabric and cut out the pieces for the kimono. Each shape is marked with the name of the piece and the dimensions for child's size 8. Draw your own diagram and fill in the measurements for your pieces.

(continued)

B
27" (68.6 cm)

Back

Belt

Band

Band

68" (172.7 cm)

A

Pocket

Belt Loops

Pocket

Right Front

left Front

Sleeve

10" (25.5cm)
D

18" (45.7cm)
E

Sleeve

13½" (34.3cm)
C

C

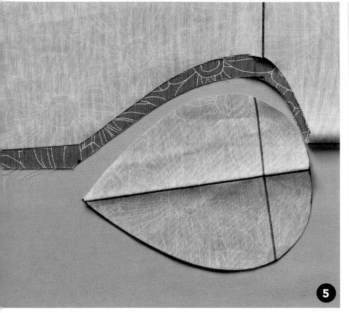

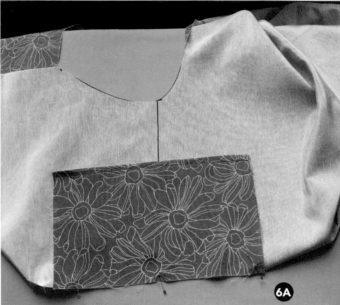

3 Smooth your fabric in a single layer, wrong side up, on the cutting surface. Cut off the selvage edges. Using a wide ruler and chalk or removable marker, carefully measure and mark your pieces on the wrong side of your fabric, following the diagram.

A Measure and mark the width and the total length (front and back) of the main garment piece. Mark the shoulder line that separates the front from the back. You will not cut on this line. Mark a line down the center separating the front into two pieces. You will cut on this line.

B Measure and mark a 4" (10 cm) strip for the belt next to the main garment piece. Its length should be equal to the garment piece.

C Draw two rectangles for the sleeves next to the band at one end of the fabric.

D Draw two 4" 910 cm) band pieces from the sleeves to the other end of the band piece.

E Draw one rectangle for the belt loops 1½" x 8" (3.8 x 20.3 cm).

F If you want pockets, draw two rectangles 5" x 6" (12.7 x 15.2 cm).

4 When you are sure your measurements and marks are correct, cut the fabric along the lines. Do not cut along the dotted shoulder line.

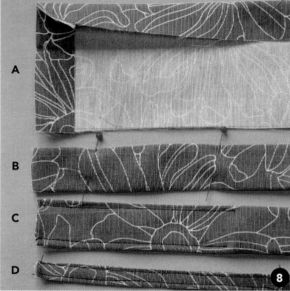

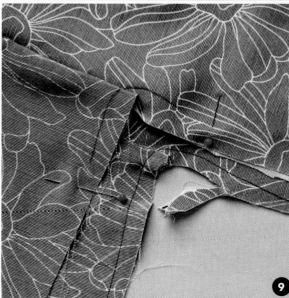

5 Fold the front/back garment piece in half the long way, right sides together. Mark 3" (7.5 cm) from the fold along the shoulder line. Divide your back length measurement in half, then measure from the shoulder line down the front cut edges and mark this measurement. Mark the center back fold 1½" (3.8 cm) from the shoulder line. Connect these marks to draw the front neckline opening, gently curving the line. Cut out the neckline.

6 Mark the center of one long edge of each sleeve. Pin a sleeve to the outer edge of the garment piece, wrong sides together, matching the center point of the sleeve to the shoulder line (A). Stitch with a ¼" (6 mm) seam allowance. Press the seam allowances toward the sleeve, and then turn the pieces right sides together so the seam is centered on the outer edge. Press, and pin again. Stitch the seam a second time using a ⅜" (1 cm) seam allowance, encasing the raw edges inside the seam (B). This is called a French seam. Press the seam allowance toward the sleeve. Repeat for the other sleeve.

7 To make the sleeve hems, fold under 1" (2.5 cm) and press. Unfold and turn the raw edge into the fold. Press, refold, and pin. Stitch close to the inner fold.

8 To make the belt, press the short ends under ½" (1.3 cm) (A). Then fold the strip in half lengthwise, wrong sides together, and press. Unfold and turn the raw edges into the center fold. Press. Refold the strip in half, and pin (B). Stitch along the folds on both sides, backtacking at the beginning and end (C). Make the belt loop strip the same way, omitting step A (D). Then cut the strip in half.

9 Lay the garment on a table, wrong sides together, aligning the front and back side edges. Pin the fronts to the back along the sides and the underside of the sleeves. At the underarm, cut the sharp corner into a curve. Stitch with a ¼" (6 mm) seam allowance from the bottom up and around the curve to the end of the sleeve.

(continued)

10 Turn right side out. Try on your kimono and mark where you want belt loops. Pin them in place. Take off the kimono. Press the seam allowances toward the back, and then turn the pieces right sides together so the seam is centered on the outer edge. Press, and pin again. Repin the belt loops from the wrong side, being sure the ends are pushed into the seam allowance. Stitch the seam a second time using a ³/₈" (1 cm) seam allowance, encasing the raw edges inside the seam. Follow the curve at the underarm and stitch twice over the belt loops. Repeat on the other side.

11 To hem the kimono, fold under 1" (2.5 cm) and press. Unfold and turn the raw edge into the fold. Press, refold, and pin. Stitch close to the inner fold.

12 To make the band, sew the two short ends of the band together, using ¼" (6 mm) seam allowance. Press the seam allowance open. Fold the band in half lengthwise, wrong sides together, and press. Unfold, and turn the raw edges into the fold. Press. Refold the strip in half.

13 Stitch ½" (1.3 cm) from the edge along the curved part of the garment neckline. This is called staystitching, and it prevents the edge from stretching out of shape. Clip the neck seam allowance to (but not through) the staystitching to allow the neckline to open into a straight line. On the wrong side, mark the center back of the neckline.

14 Aligning the seam of the band to the center back mark of the neckline, insert the neckline edge between the front and back folds of the band, overlapping the staystitching line 1/8" (3 mm). Pin through all the layers. Gently pull on the neckline edge so that it falls in a straight line, then continue to insert it between the front and back folds of the band and pin it in place. The band should lay flat with the folds pressed in place, though the garment fabric will ripple around the curve. Continue down the front of the garment on both sides, inserting the garment edge ⁵/₈" (1.6 cm) into the band and pinning often. At the ends, trim off excess leaving ½" (1.3) below the garment hem. Press the band under to match the hem length of the kimono, and pin.

15 Stitch along the inner fold of the band, taking care to catch the fold on the underside. Stitch slowly, removing pins as you go, and keeping the band flat and straight.

16 To make the pockets, fold under the top ¼" (6 mm) and stitch across (A). Fold the top down 1" (2.5 cm) to the right side, and stitch the outer edges using ⁵/₈" (1.6 cm) seam (B) to create a facing. Turn the facing to the right side, and press. Press under the sides and bottom ⁵/₈" (1.6 cm) and miter the lower corners as shown (C). Position on the front of the kimono and pin. Stitch around the pocket close to the edge, backstitching at the beginning and end. Repeat for the other pocket.

17 Thread the belt through the belt loops.

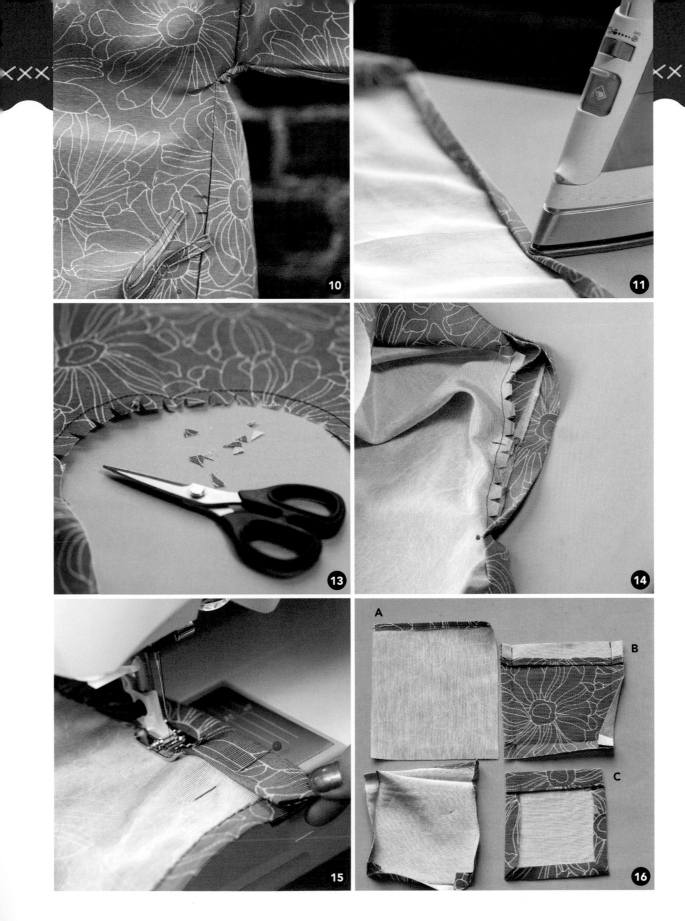

2-3
hours

Poncho

Make this fun poncho with a front zipper closure. Use laminated cotton or a fun shower curtain for a rain poncho, or choose polyester fleece for one that is warm and cozy. Sewing with special fabrics often requires a special accessory foot. For laminated cotton, use a Teflon-coated foot or put magic tape on the bottom of your regular foot to enable it to slide instead of sticking. A roller foot can be helpful when sewing on polyester fleece.

Notes:
Do not use an iron to press seams; heat damages laminated fabric or fleece.

Oilcloth is a type of laminated cotton, and can be used for this project. Be aware that the Child Product Safety Improvement Act of 2008 prohibits oilcloth garments such as bibs and aprons or toys for children under age 12.

You already know

- How to machine stitch and sew a seam allowance.
- How to make a straight hem.
- How to draw a neckline

You will learn

- More about clipping corners
- How to insert a separating zipper
- How to clip and sew on a curve

You will need

Tools

- size 80/12 needle or appropriate for the fabric you are using

- flexible measuring tape

- pins

- iron

- ruler

- press cloth

- zipper foot

- Teflon foot if using a "sticky" fabric

- roller foot if using polar fleece or thick/cushy fabrics

- marking pencil or chalk

- French curve, design ruler, or plate for drawing curves

Fabric

- 2¼ yards (2 m) laminated cotton for a poncho 26" (66 cm) long (size 8) (mid-thigh), more if your fabric has a big design

Other Supplies

- all-purpose thread

- 20" (51 cm) separating zipper, or desired length

Directions

NOTES: Seam allowance: ½" (1.3 cm) and 3/8" (1 cm)

Stitch length: 2.5 or 10 to 12 stitches per inch, 3.0 or 8 to 10 stitches per inch for topstitching

A repeat is measured from the top of a design to the top of the next design. Look at the toucans design—it has a 17½" (44.5 cm) repeat.

Stitching on laminated fabric creates holes, so stitch carefully.

The hood is cut a bit bigger to accommodate the top of the hood and ease in creating a nice finish where the zipper and hood merge.

1 Take the following measurements using a flexible measuring tape:

Poncho
Measure from wrist to wrist with your arms extended. This will be the finished width of the poncho = _____. Add 2" (5 cm) for hems_____. This will be the total cut width of the poncho back. Divide by 2. _____. (A)

Add 1" (2.5 cm) to measurement A to find the width measurement of the poncho front pieces = _____(B)

Measure how long you want it (our poncho is mid-thigh) = _____. Add ½" (1.3 cm) for shoulder seam allowance and 2" (5 cm) for lower hem. This is the length measurement of both front and back poncho pieces = _____ (C).

Hood
Measure from the hollow at the front of the neck around the face at hairline and back to the hollow. = _____ Add 10" (25.4 cm) for ease =_____Divide by 2. _____ (D)

Measure from the temple around the back of the head to the other temple. = _____Add 4" (10 cm) for ease = _____Divide by 2. = _____ (E)

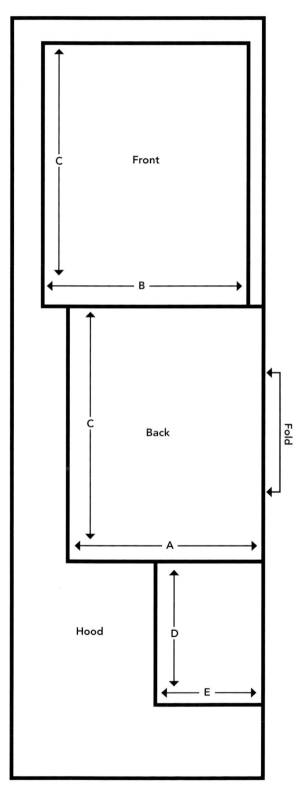

2   The diagram shows how you will mark the fabric and cut out the pieces for the poncho. Each shape is marked with the name of the piece. Draw your own diagram and fill in the measurements for your pieces.

3   Smooth your fabric in a double layer, right sides together, on the cutting surface. Trim off the selvages. Using a wide ruler and chalk or removable marker, carefully measure and mark your pieces on the wrong side of your fabric, following your diagram. Be sure to place the center back of the poncho and hood on the fold. Do not place the poncho front on the fold.

4   When you are sure your measurements and marks are correct, cut the fabric along the marked lines. Do not cut on the fold for the back and hood. Keep the pieces layered until you finish shaping the necklines in the next steps.

(continued)

5 To shape the neck on the poncho back, mark the fold 2" (5 cm) from the top; then mark the top 3" (7.5 cm) from fold. Draw a curve using a French curve, a design ruler, or a plate. Cut out the neckline. Mark the center back.

6 To shape the neck on the poncho fronts, place the fronts, right sides together on the table. Place the poncho back over the fronts, aligning the three cut edges with the back fold 1" (2.5 cm) from the right edge of the poncho fronts. Keeping the left edges aligned, slide the poncho back down 1" (2.5 cm). Your fabric will now be lined up as shown in the diagram. Trace the back neck curve onto the front, extending the lines straight to the edges as shown. Cut along the marked curve to create the poncho front necklines.

7 To shape the neck on the hood, mark the fold 5" (12.7 cm) up from the bottom. From this point, measure over 3" (7.5 cm) up and down 1" (2.5 cm) and mark a dot. This dot will line up with the shoulder seam. Mark another dot 5" (12.7 cm) from the fold and 3" (7.5 cm) up from the bottom. Lastly, place a mark 3" (7.5 cm) from the front corner. Draw a gentle S curve connecting the marks as shown. Cut the neck curve. Mark the center back of the hood and the shoulder seam dots.

8 Separate the zipper. Pin the right side of the zipper, face down, to the right front edge of the poncho, aligning the edge of the zipper to the edge of the fabric and the top of the zipper tape to the upper edge of the fabric. Using a regular presser foot, stitch from the top of the zipper tape to the bottom, guiding the edge of the foot along the edge of the zipper teeth. Pin the left side of the zipper on the other front edge, with the top of the zipper tape at the upper edge of the fabric. To sew this side in place, begin at the bottom of the zipper, so the bulk of the fabric will be to the left of the foot.

NOTE: Topstitching will be done after the hood is attached.

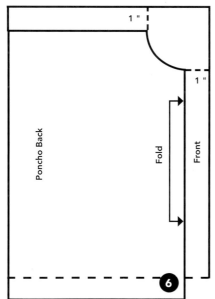

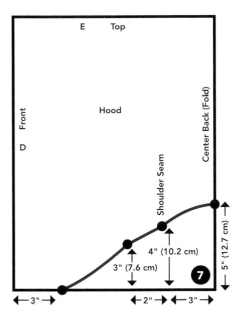

Top
E

Front

D

Hood

Center Back (Fold)

Shoulder Seam

5" (12.7 cm)

4" (10.2 cm)

3" (7.6 cm)

3"

2"

3"

7

7

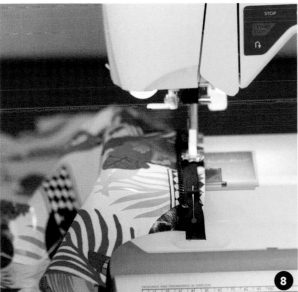

8

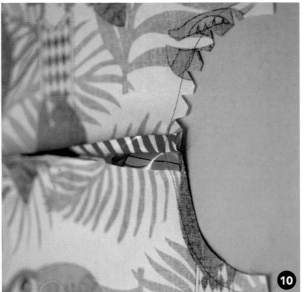

10

9 Place the poncho back and fronts right sides together. Stitch the shoulder seams with a ½" (1.3 cm) seam allowance, backtacking at the beginning and end. Press the seam allowance open using your fingers or a bamboo point turner or spoon. If the seam allowances won't stay open, you can stitch them down, guiding the edge of the presser foot along the seamline.

10 Staystitch around the poncho neckline ½" (1.3 cm) from the edge. Be sure to keep the shoulder seam allowances open flat. Clip up to the stitching line along the curves.

11 Fold the hood in half, right sides together. Stitch the top of the hood, and finger press the seam open.

(continued)

12 With right sides together, match up the marks at the center back of the hood and poncho. Stitch the hood to the poncho, matching up the shoulder seams to the marks and using a ⅝" (1.6 cm) seam allowance, clipping as needed. Note: The bottom of the hood will be larger than the neck hole. This will be trimmed later.

13 Lay out the poncho front bottom to the back bottom so all four outside corners are stacked and draw a curve for the sides, using a French curve, design ruler, or plate. Cut out the curve. If you prefer, leave the corners square.

14 Zip up the poncho to make sure the bottom is even, and trim the fabric if necessary. Unzip. Beginning at the bottom of the left front, with the wrong side of the fabric facing up, stitch ⅜" (1 cm) from the edge all the way around to the bottom of the right front. This stitching line will help you turn up the hem. Clip wedges up to the stitching line at the curves.

15 Beginning again at the bottom of the left front, with the wrong side facing up, turn the edge under ½" (1.3 cm), rolling the stitching line to the underside. Stitch the narrow hem in place, stitching ⅜" (1 cm) from the fold. Stitch slowly along the curves, stopping to ease in the excess fullness where you clipped the wedges.

16 Fold the left zipper tape to the back exposing the zipper teeth. Continue folding under the front edge the same depth to the bottom. With the right side of the fabric facing up, topstitch from the left bottom ⅜" from the fold up the front, around the hood (A), and down the right front, turning under the edge a little at a time as you sew (B).

17 Trim away the hood excess at the top of the zipper, and your poncho is ready to wear.

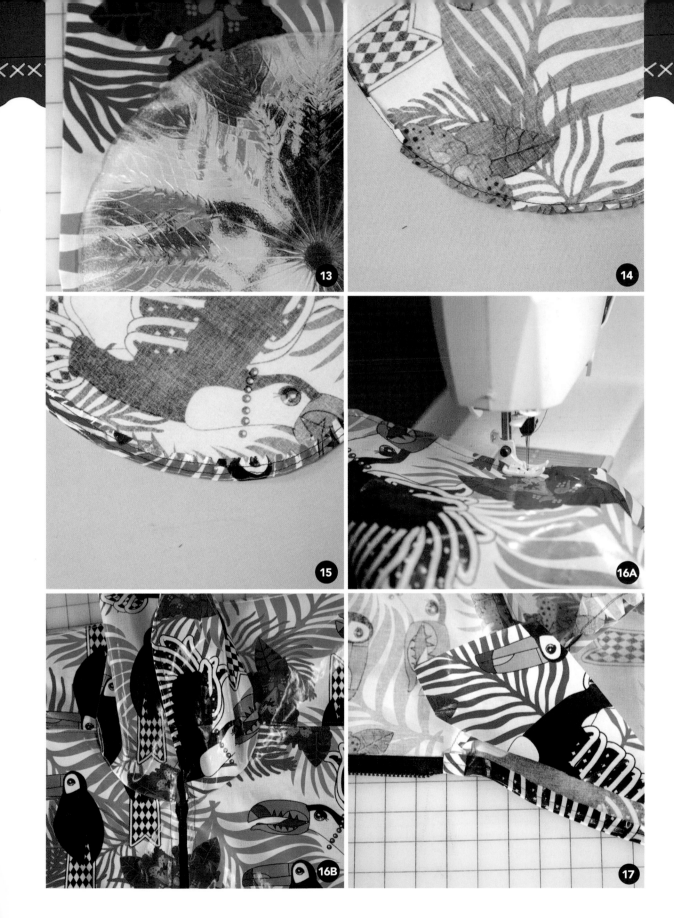

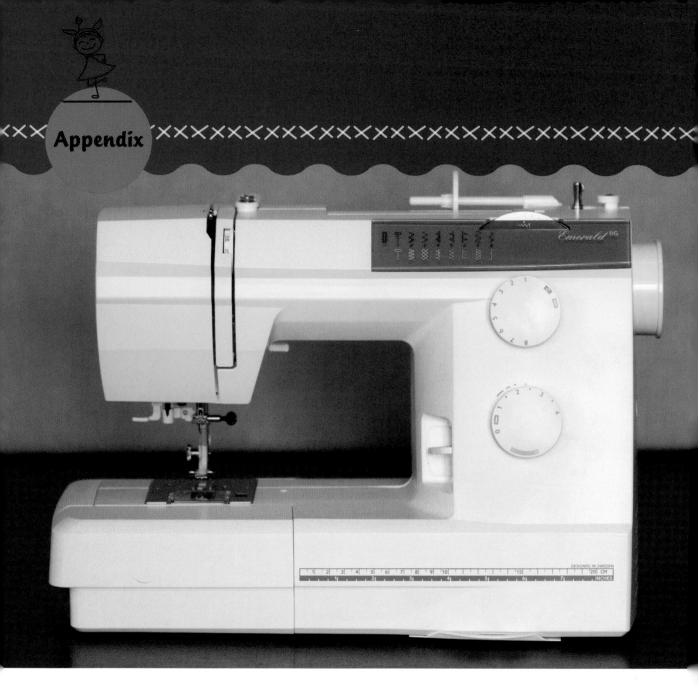

Sewing Machine

Getting to Know Your Machine

Using your manual and your machine, find the following:

Handwheel/Flywheel Located on the side of the machine, the most important thing to remember about the handwheel is that you should always turn this *toward* you. As you turn it toward you, several things move on your machine: the thread takeup lever moves, the needle goes up and down, and the feed dogs move under the presser foot. Let's take a look at each one of these more in depth.

Thread Takeup Lever This is located toward the top of the left side of the machine. When threaded, it brings the thread up and down in rhythm with the needle. The most important thing to remember about the take-up lever is that it needs to be in the highest position when you take your very first stitch and your very last stitch when sewing a seam. This indicates that you have completed the stitch cycle. If you have a computerized or an electronic machine, your machine may do this for you, but if you have a mechanical machine, you will have to turn the handwheel toward you until the take-up lever is in the up position.

Needle and Needle Screw The needle moves up and down to take a stitch when you turn the handwheel toward you. This is good to remember so that if you need to take just one or two stitches and are worried about pressing the pedal too hard, you can take those stitches with the handwheel. Needles get dull, bend, and sometimes break. We also change the needle according to which fabric/thread we are using. To replace the needle, loosen the needle screw and pull the needle down. Replace with the proper needle and hand tighten the screw. For more information about needles, including sizes and types, see page 122.

Reverse Button The reverse button does just that—it allows the machine to stitch backward. We do this for a variety reasons when sewing, such as reinforcing something, backtacking, and so on. Each reverse button looks a bit different but they function the same. Usually, you will have to hold down the button the whole time you wish to go backward. You can hold the button down and turn the handwheel toward you and see that the feed dogs now go the opposite way—they come up in the back and move toward the front of the machine, where they then drop down.

Feed Dogs The feed dogs are located under the presser foot and are what moves the fabric through the machine. They come up in the front, press the fabric against the presser foot, move it toward the back of the machine, and then lower to come forward and do it again. This is important to remember so that you are not pushing or pulling the fabric. Your job is to steer the fabric and keep it on track for where you want to sew. Let the feed dogs do the pulling. If you push or pull the fabric, you may put pressure on the needle which can result in missed stitches, bent or broken needle, and scratches on the throat plate.

Presser Foot and Presser Foot Lever The presser foot attaches to the ankle of the machine and is raised and lowered by the presser foot lever. When sewing, you will always have the presser foot lowered onto the fabric. Usually the foot you use is the utility or universal foot, but you should know that there are many different feet for uses in a variety of situations. This is a good time to find out how to take the presser foot off and put it back on again. You can also look at the accessory feet that may have come with the machine and identify them and their purpose by referring to your manual. Before sewing with a different stitch or needle position on the machine, make sure the needle will not hit the presser foot. Note: Presser feet are specific to the make and model of the machine.

Foot Pedal The foot pedal is connected to the machine by a cord and, when pressed, will cause the machine to sew or wind a bobbin. Make sure the foot pedal cord is secure in the machine. With hands in your lap (and the machine NOT threaded), practice pressing the foot pedal to control the speed of the machine. We recommend you sew barefoot or with soft-soled shoes so that you can feel the pedal easier and have more control. Place your heel on the floor with your foot two-thirds of the way up the pedal. Press lightly with the ball of your foot while keeping your heel on the floor. If you need to sew just one or two stitches, rest your foot on the pedal and curl your big toe.

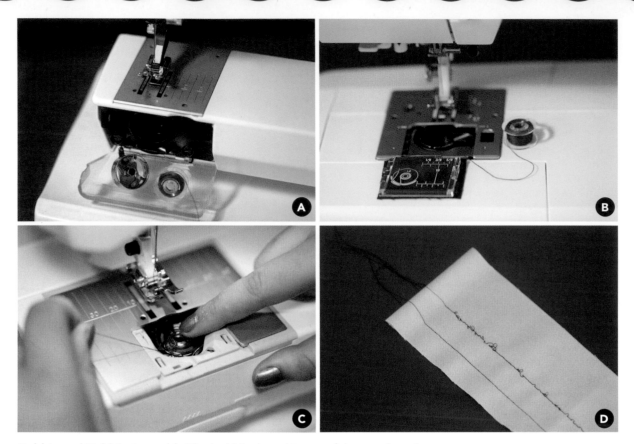

Bobbin and Bobbin Assembly The bobbin thread is one of the two threads that form the stitch. It is important that you are achieving the proper tension in the bobbin to get a good stitch. Unfortunately, most bobbins will fit in the machine both ways but will really only sew correctly one way. If you have a front-loading bobbin, you will load the bobbin case with the thread looking like the one in the photo and then drop the bobbin into the case and pull it under the tension spring (A). If you have a top-loading bobbin, you will most likely have a diagram on the cover that shows you the correct way to drop in and thread through the tension spring (B). If you place a finger on the bobbin while you pull the thread through the tension spring, you can make sure the thread is engaged in the tension spring (C). Be sure to check your owner's manual for specifics to your machine. Bobbins inserted incorrectly are a common cause of poor stitches or machines tying up. Bobbin thread that "misses" the tension spring will often be loopy on the underside of the fabric (D). In the photo, the bobbin was inserted correctly for the stitching line on the left; incorrectly for the stitching line on the right.

NOTE: Bobbins are specific to the make and model of the machine. Not all bobbins will work in all machines.

Bobbin Winder and Tension Screw The bobbin winder and tension screw are usually located on top of the sewing machine. These two are used only when winding thread onto a bobbin. It is important that you refer to your manual for exact threading to get the proper tension when winding a bobbin. Make sure the thread is engaged in the tension screw! The bobbin should wind evenly up and down the bobbin with no loose loops. Now would be a good time to wind a bobbin to use.

Stitch Pattern Selector This is where you choose which type of stitch to sew. The selector can look very different on various machines, so it is important to check your manual.

Stitch Length Selector This is where you select how long the stitch will be. If you imagine yourself walking down the street, your regular gait would equal a 2.5 on the sewing machine. This is called the standard stitch length and you will use this most often when sewing the seams. If you imagine that you are taking giant steps, then this would equal a 4 or more on the sewing machine. We often call this a basting or gathering stitch and it is a longer stitch than the standard stitch length. If you imagine yourself taking tiny steps, then this would equal a 1 on the machine and the stitches will be shorter than a standard stitch length. If you imagine yourself marching in place, this would equate to a zero on your machine and you would not have any forward motion but would be stitching in place. All of these stitch lengths have their place in sewing. The stitch length selector can look very different on various machines, so it is important to check your manual.

Stitch Width Selector When using a straight stitch, this dial often controls the needle position because a straight stitch only goes forward and doesn't have a stitch width. If you are using a zigzag or other decorative stitch, this selector determines how wide the stitch will be, or how much side-to-side motion it will have. When exploring this selector, try to find out which needle positions you have and how your machine narrows a stitch. The stitch width selector can look very different on various machines, so it is important to check your manual.

Tension Discs The machine has two metal discs that apply tension to the top thread. When the presser foot lever is up, the discs are open, so you should always thread the machine with the presser foot raised to allow the thread to slide between the discs. Lowering the presser foot also closes the tension discs. As you begin to sew beyond this book, you will explore more about the tension discs and when to adjust them. Refer to your owner's manual for more information.

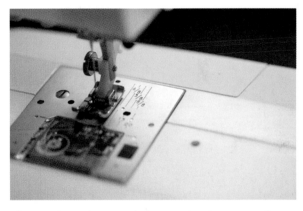

Throat Plate This metal plate under the presser foot has an oval for the needle to go through, openings for the feed dogs to come up, and seam allowance lines to help guide you. Many times these lines are marked with the common seam allowances of $3/8$" (1 cm), $1/2$" (1.3 cm), and $5/8$" (1.6 cm). You may have more lines or they may be marked on both sides of the feed dogs instead of just the right. On some machines these guidelines are for when the needle is in the center position. Some machines use the left needle position. Check your owner's manual to understand which needle position is correct for the seam allowance lines.

Accessory Feet

There are many feet designed for various purposes, but not all feet will fit your machine. It is important to know your make and model when purchasing accessory feet. Check out the feet that came with your machine and use your owner's manual to see how they work and what they do. Remember that most things can be sewn without specialty feet, but they can make it much easier and more accurate. Here are some common accessory feet.

Utility Foot (A) This foot is the go-to foot for general sewing.

Satin Stitch or Decorative Stitch Foot (B) This foot has a channel on the bottom of the foot that allows raised decorative stitches to pass through without distortion.

Zipper Foot (C) The zipper foot allows the needle to get close to the zipper teeth. On some machines you adjust the position of the needle to the right or left so it comes down in the notch on the edge of the zipper foot. For other machines, the position of the zipper foot shifts left or right and the needle stays in position.

Overcast Foot (D) The overcast foot has a finger that prevents the stitches from tugging on the edge of the fabric when sewing a seam finish.

Center Guide Foot (E) This foot has a guide bar down the center that allows you to butt the fabric up against the guide, move your needle position over to the left, and stitch a very straight topstitch.

Easy Glide Foot (F) This foot (sometimes called the Teflon foot) is used when sewing on vinyl and oilcloth to allow the foot to glide over the fabric and prevent sticking.

Buttonhole Foot (G) The buttonhole foot is used when sewing buttonholes. Your machine may have a one-step buttonhole or a four-step buttonhole foot.

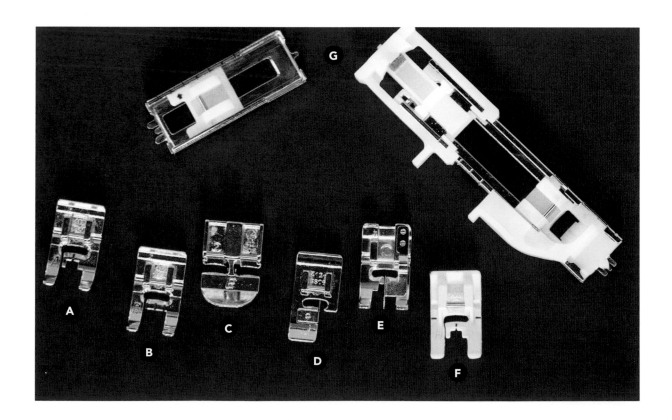

Maintenance

A note about cleaning your machine. Threads and material are made up of fibers, which can shed, leaving loose fibers and fuzz inside the machine. This can get in the way of the machine running properly. It is important to look at your owner's manual and see how to do a routine cleaning of the bobbin assembly and under the throat plate. This should be done every 10 to 12 hours of sewing or more frequently if you sew on materials that shed a lot, such as polar fleece, corduroy, velvet, etc. About three or four times a year (or more if you use your machine often) you should complete a more extensive cleaning and oil (if necessary) your machine.

Threading Your Machine

Once you have explored all the above features, you are ready to thread your machine. Most machines thread by using a combination of stationary thread guides as well as threading the take-up lever and the eye of the needle. It is important to refer to your manual for the exact threading sequence. Your machine may also be marked with reminder clues to help you. The needle is always threaded front to back and then the thread is placed through the presser foot and off to the back/side so that the presser foot sits on the thread and holds it in place when beginning a seam.

When you first change your bobbin, you need to draw your thread up through the throat plate to be ready to sew. This is also a great time to see how a stitch is formed, so check out what is happening while you do the following. After the bobbin is in place, hold the upper thread while you turn the handwheel toward you until the take-up lever goes down and up one time. This will take one stitch. Notice the upper thread goes around the bobbin to grab the bobbin thread. Pull the upper thread up through the toes of the presser foot and grasp the loop of bobbin thread that shows, pulling it up completely until you now have two thread tails: one upper thread and one bobbin thread. Now put them through the toes and under the presser foot to get ready to sew.

Tool Kit

Needles and Pins

Machine Needles (A) Needles are important to understand and as you sew you will learn more and more about why they are shaped a certain way and which needles sew best on which fabrics with which threads. For now, it is important to remember that needles are disposable. They will get dull, bend, and even break at times! You should change your needle after every eight hours of sewing, more often if you are having trouble with missed stitches or frayed and broken thread, or are sewing on specialty fabrics.

When you are sewing on woven fabrics you will use a "sharp" class of needle and when you sew on knits or things that stretch you will use a "ball" or "stretch" needle. Needles range in size, with the smaller number needles used for lighter weight fabrics while sewing with finer threads. Heavyweight fabrics use a larger needle, which can accommodate a heavier weight thread. There are also twin needles, triple needles, and double-eye needles, as well as needles for

metallics, embroidery thread, and leather, plus many, many more! You should use the correct needle for the project at hand.

Hand Needles (B) Hand needles come in all shapes and sizes. Some of the ones you use in this book include large-eye needles (crewel, chenille) that are a bit thicker in diameter and length and have a large eye to accommodate thicker threads, such as embroidery floss, and regular hand needles, which vary in size but have a smaller eye to handle regular sewing thread.

Pins: (C) Pins come in a variety of sizes with different shaped heads. Sturdy pins approximately 1¾" (4.5 cm) long with round heads are helpful when you are beginning to sew. This will give you something substantial to grasp as you learn how to pin, and they will not bend as easily as some other pins. However, they have plastic heads that will melt, so be careful when pressing. Other types of pins include glass head pins, which will not melt when used at the iron, and flower

head pins, which have larger heads that are flat and easy to see, making it easier to put a ruler over them when measuring. The flower head pins also hold lace and loosely woven fabrics without having the head slip through the holes. Whatever type of pin you use, the important thing to remember is to discard your bent and dull pins.

Needle Threader (D) If you have trouble threading your hand needles, a wire needle threader can be useful.

Magnetic Pin Cushion (E) This is a great way to store your pins. It's easy to use and great for picking up if you drop any!

Tomato Needle/Pin Holder (F) Mark needle sizes on the sections of a tomato-shaped cushion and you will always know where to find the correct needle!

Thimble (G) A thimble is used when hand sewing to protect your finger or thumb and assist in pushing the needle through the fabric.

Pattern Weights (H) These weights (sometimes felt-backed) allow you to hold your pattern in place on the fabric without pinning. They work great with a rotary cutter and mat.

Thread

Thread The type and weight of thread is chosen based on the fabric that you are using. Thread is made of fibers that are twisted together. Higher quality thread is made of fibers that are long, making the thread strong and smooth. Poorer quality thread is made of shorter fibers, which weaken it, allowing it to break and fray more easily. It can also cause the thread to have a fuzzy look, so if you use it to topstitch a seam it can look unfocused. Make sure you use a quality thread instead of bargain thread to have more success and less frustration.

Embroidery Floss Embroidery floss comes in skeins and is used in hand stitching with a large-eyed needle. You can leave the six strands together as it comes or separate it using as little as one strand at a time.

Cutting Tools

Scissors You will need two pairs of good-quality scissors in your sewing basket: one pair of angled shears approximately 8" (20 cm) long and a short pair of scissors about 5" (12.5 cm) long. The shears are used to cut your fabric and the shorter scissors are for thread cutting and smaller cuts on fabric like trimming corners. Both of these scissors should only be used on fabric! Cutting paper with them will dull them and make it hard to cut your fabric precisely. It is a good idea to have a pair of paper scissors in your tool kit as well. Snips are very small scissors that are used just for clipping threads. Zipper scissors are the pair of old scissors you use to trim across the zipper teeth. This will ruin the scissors, so it is usually the oldest pair of scissors you can find!

Rotary Cutter (A) A rotary cutter, gridded mat, and gridded ruler are used together to cut fabric with nice clean edges. This is a time-saving way to cut, but it does take a bit of practice. When you purchase a rotary cutter, it is best if you buy one that automatically retracts the blade when you release the grip. Use the grids on the mat to line up your fabric along a straight edge, lay your ruler on top of the fabric, and make sure you check that the ruler is lined up on your guidelines at the top AND the bottom. It is easy to cut a crooked line if you don't check both. To hold the ruler in place, use the pads of your finger and thumb to create five points of pressure. This will hold your

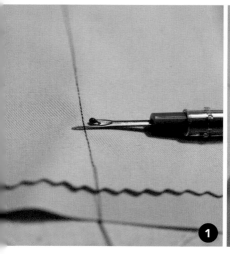

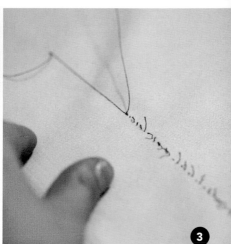

ruler in place better and be safer than placing the palm of your hand on the ruler. Press the grip of your rotary cutter and squeeze to engage the blade. Place one finger on top of the rotary cutter to gain the proper pressure as you cut. Starting just off the beginning of your fabric, place the blade flush against the ruler. Press firmly and start rolling along the ruler to cut your fabric. Use a smooth forward motion and resist sawing back and forth. You should always cut away from or across your body, never toward it. Rotary cutters are very sharp and should only be used with adult supervision.

Pinking Shears (B) Pinking shears are scissors that have a blade made up of points so that when it cuts your fabric it makes a zigzag edge. This is an easy way to finish the raw edge of your fabric to reduce fraying. Another option for pinking edges is a wave rotary cutter blade.

Seam Rippers (C) Seam rippers are used to unstitch seams that didn't sew correctly or are in the wrong spot. Seam rippers have a blade in the curved area near the pointed end and usually have a ball to protect your fabric from getting snagged. They are disposable and should be discarded when the blade becomes dull and you have to start pushing too hard to cut the thread. The best way to rip a seam—putting the least amount of stress on your fabric and leaving the smallest holes—is to lay it flat, slip the point of the seam ripper under a stitch (1), and gently push away from you to cut the threads (don't pull up on your seam ripper or you can poke your eye!). Cut every three or four stitches (and every backtack stitch) (2). Turn the fabric over and pull the thread, "unzipping" the seam (3).

Medallion Thread Cutter (D) This thread cutter is useful for removing long straight seams and can be worn as a necklace to keep something to snip threads close by. A recessed blade makes it fairly kid safe.

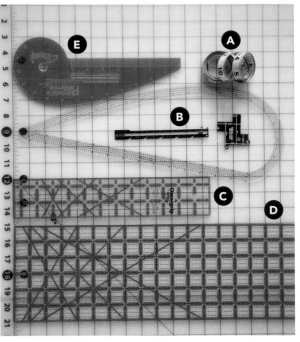

Pressing Tools

Iron and ironing board You will need a good iron and an ironing board to make your projects look as professional as possible. An iron is very hot and should only be used with adult supervision. Never leave the iron lying flat on the ironing board, as it will burn if left too long. It is important to take care not to scratch the soleplate (bottom) of your iron. An iron that steams from the bottom is preferable to one that sprays water out the front.

Pressing correctly and taking the time to do it well will do as much for your project's appearance as stitching a straight seam. Remember that before you cut your fabric, it is okay to *iron* your material, meaning you can move your iron around and slide it on top of the fabric. Once you have cut the fabric out, you will need to *press* your fabric by lifting the iron off the fabric when you move it to a different place so as not to distort or stretch the fabric.

Sleeveboard A sleeveboard is also a very useful tool to have for getting at small places and when you want to press only one layer of your project.

Press Cloth Silk organza or a polyester-organza blend is great because you can see through it and it withstands high heat. An old, clean cotton handkerchief will do in a pinch. Using a press cloth protects your fabrics and is very important when fusing interfacing because it will keep your iron clean and can be laundered.

Measuring Tools

Measuring Tape (A) A flexible 60" (152 cm) fiberglass tape measure is used to measure around the body.

Hem Gauge (B) A hem gauge is a handy tool for easy marking and can be used at the iron as well. It is easy to move the blue slider to hold your measurement.

Gridded Ruler (C) Gridded rulers come in many sizes and are usually have 1" (2.5 cm) squares to help line things up. They are easy to read and are sometimes used with rotary cutters and gridded mats. (See Rotary Cutter above.) Beware that "quilter's rulers" sometimes add ¼" (6 mm) seam allowances to the rulers.

Gridded Mat (D) A large gridded mat will help you measure accurately and "square" things up. It is a great workspace for cutting and pinning.

SA Curve Ruler and French Curve Design Ruler (E) These are special rulers to help you draw curves for necklines and armholes.

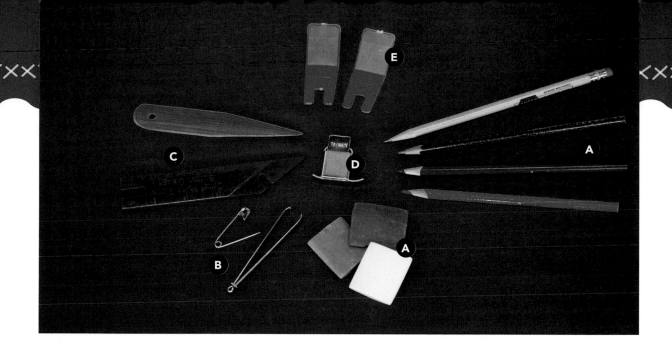

Other Handy Tools

Marking Tools (A) There are a variety of marking tools out there; some work great and others not so much. We have found that when you are marking your fabric, generally a regular pencil or colored pencil will work and comes out easily. If you are marking somewhere on your project that may show (i.e., darts, placement lines, etc.), you should use tailor's chalk, which does not have any wax in it and will brush off fabric easily. Most important is to test your marking tool on a scrap of your fabric to make sure it will come out easily.

Bodkin (B) A bodkin makes drawing a string/ribbon/elastic through a casing very easy. You attach the string at the "teeth" end and lead the bodkin through the casing with the rounded end. You can also use a safety pin.

Point Turner (C) Point turners are used to reach into corners and points to make them the proper shape. You can use the rounded side to ease curves into their natural shape as well as running along straight seams to straighten them out, thus making pressing easier. Point turners come in bamboo or plastic.

Magnetic Seam Guide (D) A magnetic seam guide can be a help if you are having difficulty staying on a certain seam allowance marking on your machine. You can place the magnetic guide at the seam allowance mark on your throat plate and butt the fabric up against it to stay on the line. Do not use magnets on computerized machines.

Hump Jumper (E) A Hump Jumper can help you go more easily over thick seams or uneven fabrics. It slips under your presser foot to raise it to the level of thick fabric and allow your machine to stitch better.

Silicone Bobbin Saver This is a great way to hold your bobbins and easily see what you have. It makes it easy to get them out without all the others falling out, too!

Tool Box A medium-size, clear plastic food container works well for a tool kit.

Standard Sewing Tool Box

Scissors
Pins
Needles
Hem gauge
Measuring tape
Thread
Marking tools
Seam ripper

Fabric and Fibers

Types

The following offers a brief description of fabrics and fibers used in this book. It by no means is a complete list of what you may find or choose to use. Pretesting is always recommended. Fabrics can be woven, knit, or felted.

Batik Light- and medium-weight cotton or rayon. Resist dyeing creates beautiful designs.

Canvas A heavy-duty woven. It can be used as a stabilizer.

Cotton A versatile woven fabric whose fibers come from the cotton plant.

Corduroy A woven fabric with ridges that run the length of the fabric. These ridges can range from very fine to a wide-wale corduroy. It is strong and wears well. The nap is important. If cutting multiple pieces, make sure the nap goes in the same direction.

Denim A strong cotton fabric. Pretreating is important.

Fashion Fabrics Fabrics used to construct garments.

Fat Quarters These are cut 18" (45.7 cm) lengthwise and 22" (56 cm) or half the width of the fabric. This is a quilting term and not to be confused with a quarter of a yard, which is 9" (23 cm) x wof (width of fabric, usually 42" to 44" (107 to 112 cm).

Felt This is a nonwoven made of pressed fibers. Wool felt is pressed with 100% wool fibers or wool and synthetic fibers. Craft felt can be thick and strong or weak and flimsy and is pressed synthetic fibers.

Fleece This synthetic material is lightweight and provides warmth. It doesn't fray or shrink.

Fusible Interfacing This material is either woven or pressed fibers with the addition of adhesive (glue). It is used to stabilize a thin material or add body and stiffness to areas of garments (such as collars and cuffs). Fusible interfacing is pressed onto the wrong side of the fabric using a hot iron and a press cloth. Enough heat and pressure are required to melt the adhesive or puckers will appear and the interfacing will not be effective.

Fusible Web This material comes in sheets or in a roll of various widths and has a paper back to protect the glue surface. It has many uses and is very helpful in appliqué work. It is fused onto the wrong side of the design, the paper is removed, and the design is then fused to the project.

Knit This nonwoven material ranges from thin T-shirt to thick sweatshirt fabric, and is stretchy.

Muslin A plain-weave fabric, muslin is usually made from cotton or a cotton blend. It is sold in a variety of qualities.

Nonwoven Fabric These materials are made of pressed fibers and have no grain lines. Examples include fleece and felt.

Oilcloth or PVC-Backed Fabric or Plastic This material has a coating over a woven fabric, making it waterproof. Use of pattern weights or low-tack tape is needed to control this fabric because pins will leave holes.

Polyester This fabric is made from synthetic fibers (petroleum-based products). Most are not biodegradable. Beware that you must use a cool/warm iron and a low dryer temperature, or polyester can melt.

Sew-in Interfacing This is an interfacing that must be sewn into the garment when making seams, unlike the fusible interfacing, which is fused with adhesive to the garment using a hot iron.

Stabilizer The many types of stabilizers all have one purpose: to give fabric support for machine embroidery or buttonholes. Stabilizers can be tear-away, cut-away, or wash-away. There are many to choose from and all offer a variety of options.

Woven Fabric This material contains warp fibers (threads put onto a loom before the fabric is woven) and weft fibers (threads woven across and through the warp fibers).

Working with Fabric

Raw Edge The raw edge of fabric is the cut edge, and this is prone to fraying or unraveling. Take care to finish off the raw edges.

Selvage (or Selvedge) The selvage is the edge of the fabric. Some selvage edges are printed with information about the manufacturer or company or even offer little dots displaying the colors used in the fabric. The selvages are often more tightly woven and can shrink at a different rate from the fabric, so they should be cut off and not used as part of a project.

Directional Designs If you are working with a print, take a careful look at the direction of the design. Designs can go one way (such as letters), two ways (such as stripes), or in any direction (such as polka dots). The distance from one design to the next is called a repeat.

Nap This is a texture on the surface of the fabric. It is smooth in one direction and rough in the opposite direction. Make sure the nap goes in the same direction when piecing fabric together.

Grain Line The grain line describes the direction in which the fibers line up in the fabric. It's important to cut out pieces from material in the way the pattern directs, because it will affect how much the fabric stretches. Straight of grain means the cuts are made parallel to the selvage edge, and this will give the strongest piece of material with little, if any, stretch. Cross grain means the cuts are made from selvage edge to selvage edge (the opposite of straight of grain) and has a bit of stretch. Bias means cutting on the diagonal of the fabric (corner to corner), and it has the most stretch.

Pretreating It's important to wash and dry a fabric before you use it because most fabrics shrink. Less expensive fabrics have a "sizing," or stiffening agent such as starch, added to them. Sizing washes out, often leaving fabrics thin and limp and not acceptable for certain projects. Some fabrics may need to be dry-cleaned, depending on the fiber.

Zippers If your project calls for a zipper, it will specify which type of zipper to use. All-purpose zippers (right) do not separate at the bottom, and they come in different weights to suit the project. Separating zippers (left) come apart in two pieces for projects like the poncho on page 108. Zippers like the white one shown have teeth that are intended to be exposed.

You can shorten an all-purpose zipper by creating a new zipper stop at the desired length. Center the closed zipper under the presser foot, set the machine stitch length to 0 and the stitch width to the widest setting. Using your handwheel, zigzag five times over the zipper teeth to create a bar tack. Trim the excess zipper tape using an old scissors.

PARTS OF A ZIPPER

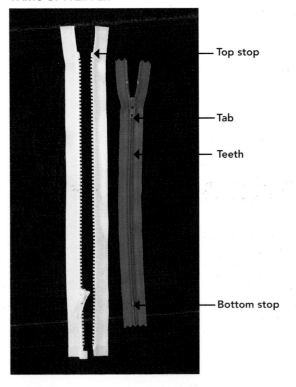

- Top stop
- Tab
- Teeth
- Bottom stop

Sources

Annie's Crafts
www.anniescatalog.com
Sewing and craft supplies

Auger's & Sons
www.augerandsons.com
Service and repairs

Designs by Janith
www.designsbyjanith.com
Brass pattern weights

Husqvarna
http://new.husqvarnaviking.com/en-US/Machines/
OPAL-650
Viking Opal sewing machine

Kai scissors
www.kaiscissors.com
Quality scissors

Nancy's Notions
www.nancysnotions.com
Sewing supplies

Olfa
www.olfa.com/splash.aspx
Quality rotary cutters

Pamela's Patterns
www.pamelaspatterns.com
Design Ruler

Rowenta
www.rowentausa.com
Quality irons

Schmetz needles
www.schmetzneedles.com
Quality needles

SSN Designs
www.ssndesigns.com
Hump Jumper

The Sewing Tree
www.thesewingtree.com
Sewing classes for those in the Dover,
New Hampshire, area

Threads Magazine
www.threadsmagazine.com
Magazine about all things sewing

The Wooly Thread
www.woolythread.com
SA Curve Rulers

Acknowledgments

We are thankful for all of our students. Your enthusiasm and excitement empower us to continue teaching. Every student with a question has offered us an opportunity to learn how to teach.

We would also like to thank our wonderful husbands and amazing children for their support of our passion for teaching sewing. Without them, we could not possibly do what we do.

About the Authors

Janith Bergeron

Christine Ecker

Janith Bergeron and Christine Ecker founded The Sewing Tree in the spring of 2003 and enjoy teaching sewing to people of all ages and interests. They have developed a very comprehensive method of teaching from beginner to advanced students.

Janith Bergeron, proprietress of Designs by Janith, founded in 1991, specializes in creating beautiful, custom-designed garments. She teaches classes at various sewing-related businesses and schools, striving to bring fun into every stitch and a sense of accomplishment into every project. Janith was the founder of the New Hampshire chapter of the American Sewing Guild in 2001. A Master Certified Sewing Educator-SEA (2008), a Trained Sewing Educator/S&CA since 2002, and a 4-H educator/leader, Janith has been a contributor to *Threads* magazine's Pattern Review since 2003. Janith lives in Barrington, New Hampshire.

Freddy Ecker

Christine Ecker began sewing as a young child with her grandmother and cherishes a yellow sundress that was one of her early projects. Christine is primarily self-taught and her sewing interests include specialty dresses, costumes, children's clothes, home decor, crafts, bags, and machine embroidery. As the owner of Stolen Time Creations, Christine worked closely with a local Portsmouth, New Hampshire designer creating one-of-a-kind handbags. Christine was an active member of the board for the New Hampshire chapter of the American Sewing Guild. She has been a Trained Sewing Educator/S&CA since 2004. Christine lives in Dover, New Hampshire with her husband and four children. Bella and Freddy Ecker served as hand models for the sewing steps.

Bella Ecker

Straight Stitch Template

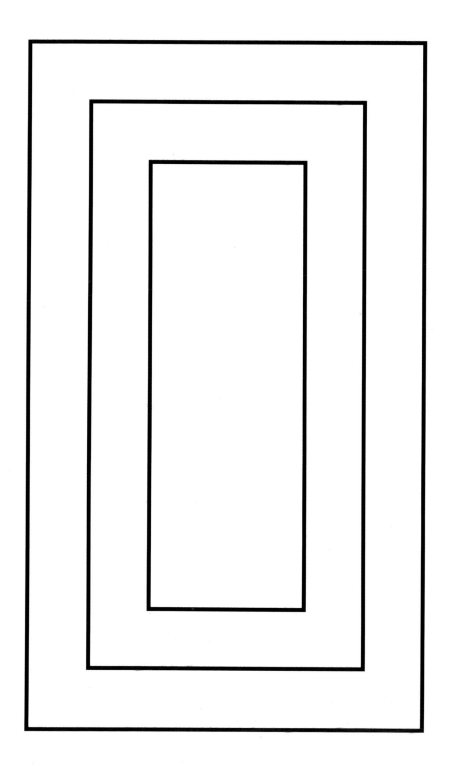

Slow Curve Template

Flower Power Patterns

Fold tracing paper in half and align fold to dashed line. Trace pattern and cut through both layers to make pattern with five petals.

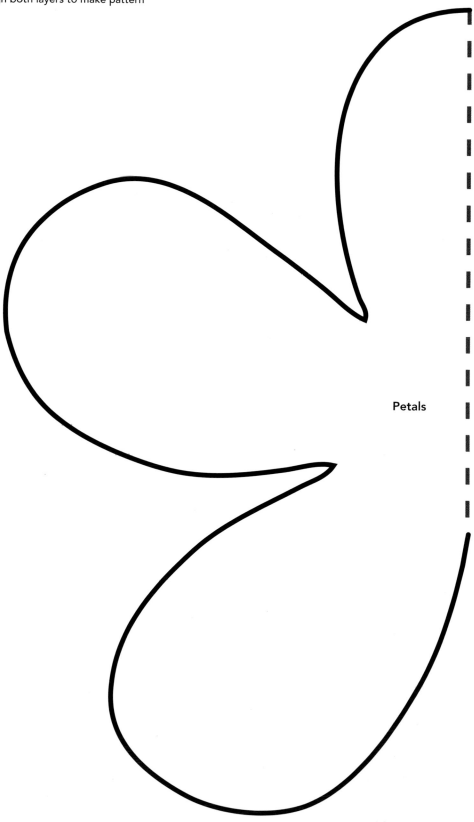

Petals

Tooth Fairy Pillow Patterns

Fold tracing paper in half and align fold to dashed line.
Trace pattern and cut through both layers to make pattern.

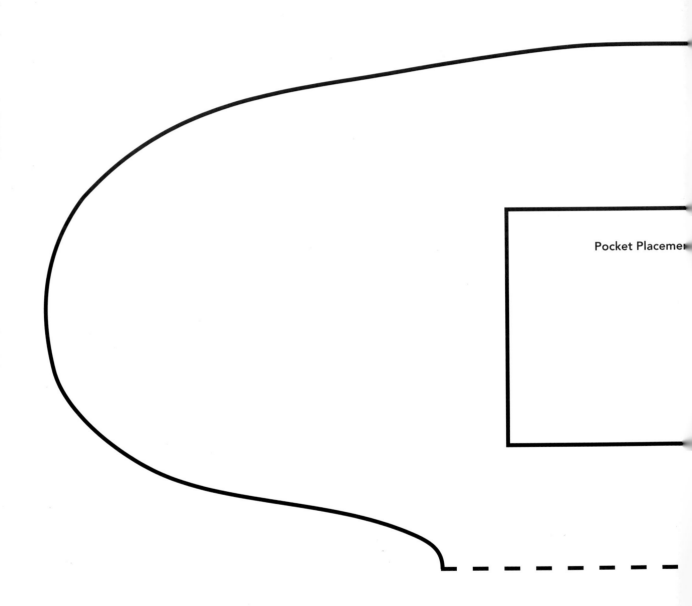

Pocket Placemer

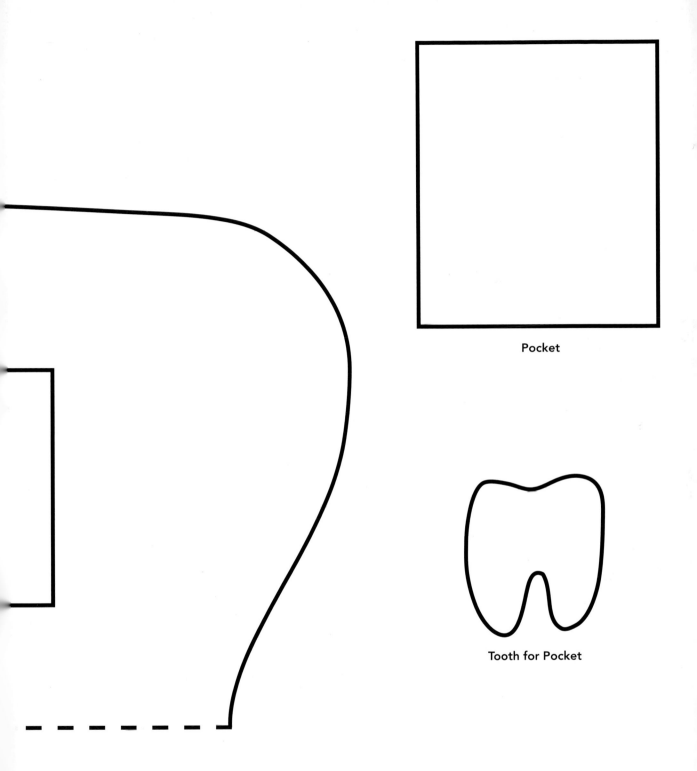

Pocket

Tooth for Pocket

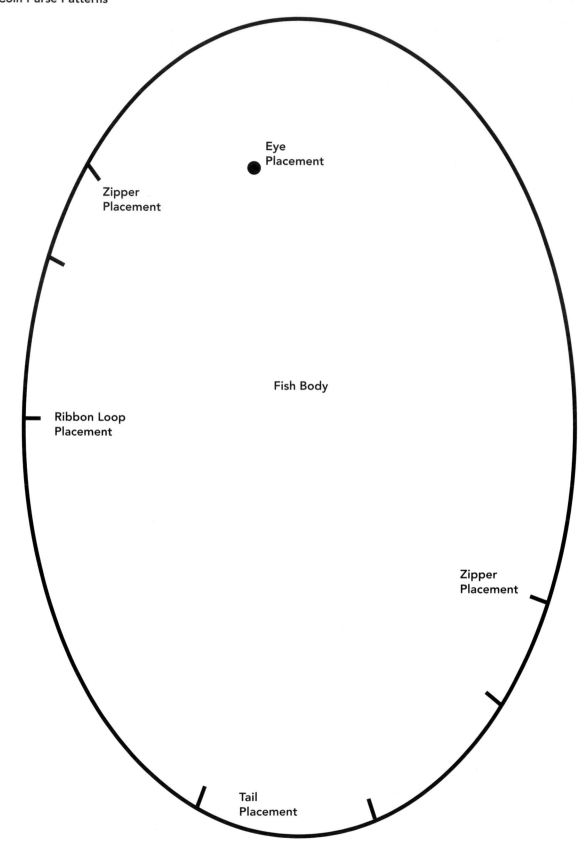

Eye Placement

Zipper Placement

Fish Body

Ribbon Loop Placement

Zipper Placement

Tail Placement

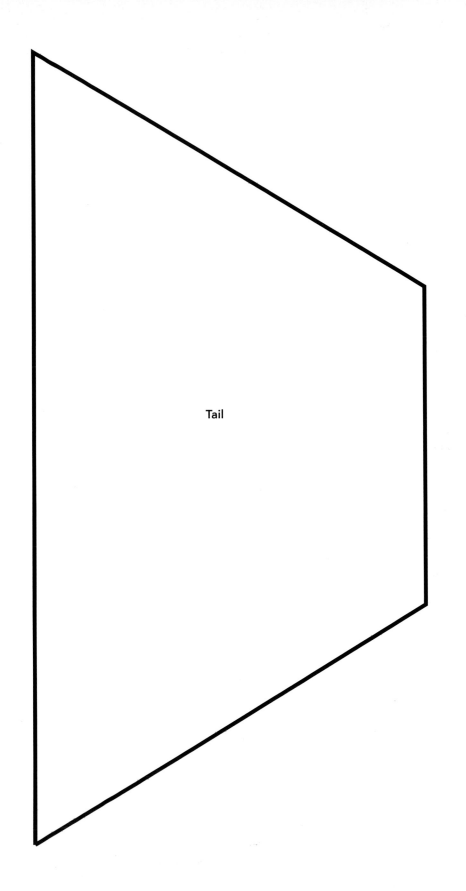

Tail

Index

Index (continued)